SO-AJO-335

Children's Learning in the "Zone of Proximal Development"

Barbara Rogoff, James V. Wertsch, *Editors*

NEW DIRECTIONS FOR CHILD DEVELOPMENT
WILLIAM DAMON, *Editor-in-Chief*

Number 23, March 1984

Paperback sourcebooks in
The Jossey-Bass Social and Behavioral Sciences Series

Jossey-Bass Inc., Publishers
San Francisco • Washington • London

Barbara Rogoff, James V. Wertsch (Eds.).
Children's Learning in the "Zone of Proximal Development."
New Directions for Child Development, no. 23.
San Francisco: Jossey-Bass, 1984.

New Directions for Child Development Series
William Damon, *Editor-in-Chief*

Copyright © 1984 by Jossey-Bass Inc., Publishers
and
Jossey-Bass Limited

Copyright under International, Pan American, and Universal
Copyright Conventions. All rights reserved. No part of
this issue may be reproduced in any form — except for brief
quotation (not to exceed 500 words) in a review or professional
work — without permission in writing from the publishers.

New Directions for Child Development (publication number
USPS 494-090) is published quarterly by Jossey-Bass Inc., Publishers.
Second-class postage rates are paid at San Francisco, California,
and at additional mailing offices.

Correspondence:
Subscriptions, single-issue orders, change of address notices, undelivered
copies, and other correspondence should be sent to Subscriptions,
Jossey-Bass Inc., Publishers, 433 California Street, San Francisco
California 94104.

Editorial correspondence should be sent to the Editor-in-Chief,
William Damon, Department of Psychology, Clark University,
Worcester, Massachusetts 01610.

Library of Congress Catalogue Card Number LC 83-82716
International Standard Serial Number ISSN 0195-2269
International Standard Book Number ISBN 87589-983-8

Cover art by Willi Baum
Manufactured in the United States of America

55.413
C437

L.I.F.E. College Library
1100 Glendale Blvd.
Los Angeles, Calif. 90026

Ordering Information

The paperback sourcebooks listed below are published quarterly and can be ordered either by subscription or single-copy.

Subscriptions cost $35.00 per year for institutions, agencies, and libraries. Individuals can subscribe at the special rate of $25.00 per year *if payment is by personal check.* (Note that the full rate of $35.00 applies if payment is by institutional check, even if the subscription is designated for an individual.) Standing orders are accepted. Subscriptions normally begin with the first of the four sourcebooks in the current publication year of the series. When ordering, please indicate if you prefer your subscription to begin with the first issue of the *coming* year.

Single copies are available at $8.95 when payment accompanies order, and *all single-copy orders under $25.00 must include payment.* (California, New Jersey, New York, and Washington, D.C., residents please include appropriate sales tax.) For billed orders, cost per copy is $8.95 plus postage and handling. (Prices subject to change without notice.)

Bulk orders (ten or more copies) of any individual sourcebook are available at the following discounted prices: 10–49 copies, $8.05 each; 50–100 copies, $7.15 each; over 100 copies, *inquire.* Sales tax and postage and handling charges apply as for single copy orders.

To ensure correct and prompt delivery, all orders must give either the *name of an individual* or an *official purchase order number.* Please submit your order as follows:

Subscriptions: specify series and year subscription is to begin.
Single Copies: specify sourcebook code (such as, CD8) and first two words of title.

Mail orders for United States and Possessions, Latin America, Canada, Japan, Australia, and New Zealand to:
Jossey-Bass Inc., Publishers
433 California Street
San Francisco, California 94104

Mail orders for all other parts of the world to:
Jossey-Bass Limited
28 Banner Street
London EC1Y 8QF.

New Directions for Child Development Series
William Damon, *Editor-in-Chief*

CD1 *Social Cognition,* William Damon
CD2 *Moral Development,* William Damon
CD3 *Early Symbolization,* Howard Gardner, Dennie Wolf
CD4 *Social Interaction and Communication During Infancy,* Ina C. Uzgiris
CD5 *Intellectual Development Beyond Childhood,* Deanna Kuhn
CD6 *Fact, Fiction, and Fantasy in Childhood,* Ellen Winner, Howard Gardner

032666

Contents

Editors' Notes

In American psychology, research and theory on cognitive development have been dominated by an examination of the individual's development as if it occurred in isolation from other people and the larger cultural context. In recent years, developmentalists have become interested in Vygotsky's (1962, 1978) theory, which stresses that cognitive functioning occurs first on the social level, between people, and that the child then internalizes this in individual development. Of special interest is Vygotsky's concept of the zone of proximal development (zona blizhaishego razvitiya). The Russian word *blizhaishego* is the superlative form of the word for *close*. Hence, the literal translation of *zona blizhaishego razvitiya* is *zone of closest* or *nearest development*. In this volume however, we continue the practice of using the phrase *zone of proximal development* to translate this term. Vygotsky's concept focuses on the phase in development in which the child has only partially mastered a task but can participate in its execution with the assistance and supervision of an adult or more capable peer. The zone of proximal development is this a dynamic region of sensitivity in which cognitive development advances. In these editor's notes, we provide some background on Vygotsky's theory to aid readers in understanding his notion of the zone of proximal development. We then describe the uses to which the concept has been put in recent developmental literature in the West as well as in the chapters presented in this volume.

The Zone of Proximal Development in the Context of Vygotsky's Theory

The Soviet psychologist and semiotician Lev Semenovich Vygotsky (1896–1934) attempted to formulate a theory of psychology built on the foundation of Marxism. Fundamental to his theory was the idea that higher mental functions, such as thinking, voluntary attention, and logical memory, and human consciousness in general have their origins in human social life, deriving from "internalized social relations that have become functions for the individual and forms of his/her structure" (Vygotsky, 1981, p. 164). Vygotsky was critical of approaches to psychology that place primary focus on investigating individual functioning and assume that collective function is derivative of it. Instead, he argued that the primary focus should be "to show how the individual response emerges from the form of collective life" (1981, p. 165). In other words, analysis of the ontogenesis of cognitive functioning requires studying how children's social interaction with more experienced members of their culture is mastered and internalized.

Vygotsky's (1981) "general law of the development of higher mental functions" postulated that mental functioning occurs first between people in

1

social interaction and then within the child on the psychological plane. This implies that mental functions, such as thinking, reasoning, problem solving, or logical memory, can be carried out in collaboration by several people (on the interpsychological plane) as well as by an individual (on the intrapsychological plane). That is, dyads or groups as well as individuals can be agents that think and remember.

Vygotsky's formulation claims, furthermore, that the very structure of individual functioning derives from and reflects the structure of social functioning. Thus, his claim is much stronger than simply that individuals' mental processes develop in a social milieu. That is, Vygotsky views individuals' mental processes as having specific organizational properties that reflect those of the social life from which they derive. The composition, structure, and means of action are internalized from their social origins. This means that variation in the organization of social functioning can be expected to lead to variation in the organization of individual psychological functioning. For example, a child who has participated in joint problem solving will use the same task representation that proved effective in group problem solving when solving such a problem independently. Hence, Vygotsky's approach suggests that to understand individual cognitive growth it will be fruitful to examine specific patterns of social interaction in which children participate.

It was in the course of applying these theoretical concepts to practical problems in cognitive and educational psychology that Vygotsky introduced the notion of the zone of proximal development. He was concerned with the relationship between two levels of development: a child's level of individual, independent functioning (the level of "actual development") and the level at which he or she can function while participating in instructional social interaction (the level of "potential development"). It is these two levels of task performance that define the boundaries of the zone of proximal development.

Many of Vygotsky's comments about the zone of proximal development derive from his critique of psychological testing. He criticized the practice of focusing on "where a child has been" (that is, on the child's level of actual development) to the exclusion of the child's potential for growth. He specified the level of actual development as "the level of a child's development of mental functions which has taken shape as a result of specific, already completed cycles of his or her development. In essence, when we determine the mental age of a child with the help of tests we are almost always concerned with the level of actual development" (1956, p. 446).

According to Vygotsky, a separate assessment of the level of potential development is necessary, because it can vary independently of the level of actual development. He provided the following hypothetical example: "Imagine that we have examined two children and determine that the mental age of both is seven years. This means that both children solve tasks accessible to seven-year-olds. However, when we attempt to push these children further in carrying out the tests, there turns out to be an essential difference between them.

With the help of leading questions, examples, and demonstrations, one of them easily solves test items taken from two years above his level of [actual] development. The other solves test items that are only a half year above his level of [actual] development" (1956, pp. 446–447). Was the mental development of the two children equivalent? Vygotsky suggests that the answer depends on which level of task performance one measures — the individual level or the collaborative level: "From the point of view of their independent activity they are equivalent, but from the point of view of their immediate potential development they are sharply different. That which the child turns out to be able to do with the help of an adult points us toward the zone of his or her proximal development. This means that with the help of this method we can take stock not only of today's completed process of development, not only the cycles that are already concluded and done; we can also take stock of processes which are now in the state of coming into being, are only ripening, or are only developing" (1956, pp. 447–448).

Vygotsky's concern with assessing both the child's actual and potential developmental levels has grown into a philosophy of testing in the Soviet Union that is beginning to influence the U.S. literature on assessment. There is growing interest in examining the difference between a child's performance on a task when unassisted and when given a graduated series of supports for problem solving (for example, Brown and French, 1979).

There was another aspect, however, of Vygotsky's interest in the zone of proximal development. Concern with the relationship between a child's level of actual development and level of potential development led to considerations of the appropriate level of collaborative functioning for a child. For a child to profit from joint cognitive activity, such activity must be geared appropriately to the child's level of potential development, thereby advancing the child's level of actual development. Vygotsky criticized the view of instruction that is based on an assumption that "instruction must be oriented toward stages that have already been completed" (1956, p. 448). He argued instead that "*instruction is good only when it proceeds ahead of development. It then awakens and rouses to life those functions which are in a stage of maturing, which lie in the zone of proximal development. It is in this way that instruction plays an extremely important role in development*" (1956, p. 278). (The Russian word *obuchenie,* which is here translated as *instruction,* has no precise equivalent in English. It covers the notion of teaching as well as the notion of learning. Hence, a more accurate but entirely too cumbersome translation is *teaching-learning process.* In English, *instruction* often focuses primarily on teaching, but since it can be understood to cover both teaching and learning, it seems to be the best translation. The important point is that *obuchenie* does not refer to one or the other aspect of the teaching-learning process in isolation. Rather, it recognizes both as parts of a whole.)

In his discussion of the role of instruction in leading development, Vygotsky specified that the form of joint cognitive activity is internalized to become the structure of the child's independent cognitive functioning: "[Instruction] rouses to life, awakens, and sets in motion a variety of internal processes of development in the child. At this point, these processes are still possible for the child only in the sphere of interaction with surrounding people and in the sphere of collaboration with peers. But these processes, which constitute the course of internal development, then become the internal property of the child himself or herself" (1956, p. 450).

The zone of proximal development serves a central role in Vygotsky's theory as an essential means through which the social world guides the child in development of individual functions. The use of the tools and techniques of society are introduced to the child and practiced in social interaction with more experienced members of society in the zone of proximal development. Vygotsky's formulation of the zone of proximal development has begun to spark considerable interest in the West, as it seems to offer a promising perspective for the consideration of many problems that challenge developmental and educational psychologists today.

The Concept of the Zone of Proximal Development in Current Research

While a brief introduction to Vygotsky's concept of the zone of proximal development is available in Chapter Six of *Thought and Language* (1962), it was only when a more extended treatement became available in translation (1978) that American investigators began to appreciate the potential of this notion. An exception to this is found in the work of Wood and Bruner and their colleagues (Wood, 1980; Wood and others, 1976; Wood and others, 1978). They developed the closely related notion of "scaffolding," a process wherein an adult provides support to a child learning to master a problem.

This and other related research in the West has begun to identify a number of processes in individual functioning that appear to be facilitated by social guidance. For example, the argument has been applied to language and skill acquisition (Bruner, 1975; Greenfield, in press; Kaye and Charney, 1980; Scollon, 1976; Zukow and others, 1982) the production of narrative (McNamee, 1981), to reading (Au and Kawakami, in press; Cazden, 1979; Tharp and others, in press), to the development of game scripts (Hodapp and Goldfield, 1983; Zukow, 1983), to memory (Rogoff and Gardner, in press), and to problem solving (Ellis and Rogoff, in press; Wertsch, 1979). These applications of the notion of the zone of proximal development have included children from infancy to adolescence.

While Vygotsky himself was most concerned with instruction in school, the recent research on the zone of proximal development that extends Vygotsky's ideas to a wider range of mental functions, ages, and settings is quite consistent with his ideas. He argued that "we must understand *the general relationship that exists between instruction in development in general*" as well as "*the specific properties of this relationship during the school-age years*" (1956, p. 446). The work reported in this volume focuses on the mental functions of numerical understanding, game and tool use scripts, problem solving, and reasoning. It includes work with infants, preschoolers, school-age children, and adolescents observed at home, at school, at work, and in the laboratory.

Each chapter provides elaboration of the theoretical concept of the zone of proximal development, with convergence across the chapters in the themes that can fruitfully extend Vygotsky's seminal notion. Most of the chapters deal with all three of the following primary themes: First, the zone of proximal development involves the joint consciousness of the participants, where two or more minds are collaborating on solving a problem. A corollary of this notion of intersubjectivity is that the participants do not have the same definition of the task or of the problem to be solved. Through their interaction, the child's notion of what is to be done goes beyond itself, with the adult's support, and comes to approximate in some degree that of the more expert adult. Second, both participants play an important role in using the zone of proximal development, even in situations that are not directly conceived of as instructional by the participants. The child provides skills that are already developing and interests in particular domains and participates with the adult in organizing the direction and pace of interaction in the zone of proximal development. The adult has particular responsibility for segmenting the task into manageable subgoals and for altering the child's definition of the task to make it increasingly compatible with expert performance. Although intervention and assessment can be finely tuned to match the growing edge of the child's competence, there are circumstances in which what the child is encouraged or allowed to do does not fit the child's immediate potential growth. Third, interaction in the zone of proximal development is organized into a dynamic functional system oriented toward the child's future skills and knowledge. The functional system of adult-child joint participation in problem solving is organized by the task definitions, promoted activities, and hard and soft technologies available through culture.

James V. Wertsch
Barbara Rogoff
Editors

References

Au, K. H., and Kawakami, A. J. "Vygotskian Perspectives on Discussion Processes in Small Group Reading Lessons." In L. C. Wilkinson, P. L. Peterson, and M. Hallinan (Eds.), *Student Diversity and the Organization, Processes, and Use of Instructional Groups in the Classroom.* New York: Academic Press, in press.

Brown, A. L., and French, L. A. "The Zone of Proximal Development: Implications for Intelligence Testing in the Year 2000." *Intelligence,* 1979, *3,* 255–277.

Bruner, J. "From Communication to Language: A Psychological Perspective." *Cognition,* 1975, *3,* 255–287.

6

Cazden, C. "Peekaboo as an Instructional Model: Discourse Development at Home and at School." In *Papers and Reports on Child Language Development*. No. 17. Stanford, Calif.: Department of Linguistics, Stanford University, 1979.

Ellis, S., and Rogoff, B. "Problem Solving in Children's Management of Instruction." In E. Mueller and C. Cooper (Eds.), *Process and Outcome in Peer Relationships*. New York: Academic Press, in press.

Greenfield, P. M. "A Theory of the Teacher in the Learning Activities of Everyday Life." In B. Rogoff and J. Lave (Eds.), *Everyday Cognition: Its Development in Social Context*. Cambridge, Mass.: Harvard University Press, in press.

Hodapp, R. M., and Goldfield, E. C. "Self Versus Other Regulation in the Infancy Period." Unpublished manuscript, Yale University, 1983.

Kaye, K., and Charney, R. "How Mothers Maintain 'Dialogue' with Two-Year-Olds." In D. Olson (Ed.), *The Social Foundations of Language and Thought: Essays in Honor of Jerome S. Bruner*. New York: Norton, 1980.

McNamee, G. D. "Social Origins of Narrative Skills." Paper presented at the meetings of the Society for Research in Child Development, Boston, April 1981.

Rogoff, B., and Gardner, W. P. "Adult Guidance of Cognitive Development." In B. Rogoff and J. Lave (Eds.), *Everyday Cognition: Its Development in Social Context*. Cambridge, Mass.: Harvard University Press, in press.

Scollon, R. *Conversations with a One-Year-Old*. Honolulu: University Press of Hawaii, 1976.

Tharp, R. G., Jordan, C., Speidel, G. E., Au, K. H., Klein, T. W., Calkins, R. P., Sloat, K. C. M., and Gallimore, R. "Product and Process in Applied Developmental Research: Education and the Children of a Minority." In M. E. Lamb, A. L. Brown, and B. Rogoff (Eds.), *Advances in Developmental Psychology*. Vol. 3. Hillsdale, N.J.: Erlbaum, in press.

Vygotsky, L. S. *Selected Psychological Investigations*. Moscow: Izdstel'sto Akademii Pedagogicheskikh Nauk SSSR, 1956.

Vygotsky, L. S. *Thought and Language*. Cambridge, Mass.: M.I.T. Press, 1962.

Vygotsky, L. S. *Mind in Society: The Development of Higher Psychological Processes*. Cambridge, Mass.: Harvard University Press, 1978.

Vygotsky, L. S. "The Genesis of Higher Mental Functions." In J. V. Wertsch (Ed.), *The Concept of Activity in Soviet Psychology*. Armonk, N.Y.: Sharpe, 1981.

Wertsch, J. V. "From Social Interaction to Higher Psychological Processes: A Clarification and Application of Vygotsky's Theory." *Human Development*, 1979, *22*, 1–22.

Wood, D. J. "Teaching the Young Child: Some Relationships Between Social Interaction, Language, and Thought." In D. R. Olson (Ed.), *The Social Foundations of Language and Thought*. New York: Norton, 1980.

Wood, D., Bruner, J. S., and Ross, G. "The Role of Tutoring in Problem Solving." *Journal of Child Psychology and Psychiatry*, 1976, *17*, 89–100.

Wood, D., Wood, H., and Middleton, D. "An Experimental Evaluation of Four Face-to-Face Teaching Strategies." *International Journal of Behavioral Development*, 1978, *2*, 131–147.

Zukow, P. G. "The Relationship Between Interaction with the Caregiver and the Emergence of Play Activities During the One-Year Period." Unpublished manuscript, University of Southern California, 1983.

Zukow, P. G., Reilly, J., and Greenfield, P. M. "Making the Absent Present: Facilitating the Transition from Sensorimotor to Linguistic Communication." In K. Nelson (Ed.), *Children's Language*. Vol. 3. New York: Gardner Press, 1982.

James V. Wertsch is associate professor and chair, Department of Linguistics, Northwestern University, and research fellow at the Center for Psychosocial Studies.

Barbara Rogoff is associate professor of developmental psychology, University of Utah.

Vygotsky's ideas about the zone of proximal development are elucidated and extended by inclusion of the theoretical constructs of situation definition, intersubjectivity, and semiotic mediation.

The Zone of Proximal Development: Some Conceptual Issues

James V. Wertsch

As the work reported in this volume shows, Vygotsky's notion of the zone of proximal development has recently spurred a great deal of interest among developmental and cognitive psychologists. His ideas have been incorporated into studies on a variety of issues, including intelligence testing (for example, Brown and Ferrara, in press; and the chapter by Campione, Brown, Ferrara, and Bryant in this volume), memory (for example, Rogoff and Gardner, in press), and problem solving (for example, Wertsch, 1979; Wertsch and others, 1980).

As we come to consider more and more psychological phenomena from the perspective of the zone of proximal development, it becomes increasingly important to explicate this theoretical construct. Failure to do so raises the risk that it will be used loosely and indiscriminately, thereby becoming so amorphous that it loses all explanatory power. In what follows, I shall identify some aspects of Vygotsky's account of the zone of proximal development that are in need of clarification, and I shall undertake this clarification by extending his ideas in light of contemporary theoretical and empirical research.

This chapter is based on a presentation at the biennual meetings of the Society for Research in Child Development, Detroit, 1983.

B. Rogoff, J. V. Wertsch (Eds.). *Children's Learning in the "Zone of Proximal Development."*
New Directions for Child Development, no. 23. San Francisco: Jossey-Bass, March 1984.

Recall that Vygotsky defined the zone of proximal development as *"the distance between the actual developmental level as determined by independent problem solving and the level of potential development as determined through problem solving under adult guidance or in collaboration with more capable peers"* (1978, p. 86). Vygotsky made several additional general comments about the zone of proximal development, but nowhere in his writing did he provide an account of what constitutes "problem solving under adult guidance or in collaboration with more capable peers." In the absence of such an account, the level of potential development, and hence the zone of proximal development in general, cannot be defined in any precise way.

As an example of the difficulties that arise if one fails to provide a precise, concrete analysis of the level of potential development, consider the case of an adult helping a fifth-grader to carry out the problem of dividing 124 by 23. In such a case, we might expect such adult utterances as "How many times will 23 go into 124?" or "What do you do with the remainder?" That is, we could expect leading questions about divisors, dividends, remainders, and so forth. Now, compare this with the case of an adult who helps a first-grader to solve the same problem by telling him or her to write certain numbers in certain locations on a sheet of paper. In this case, we might expect such utterances as "Now put a four up here right after the five." If the problem is completed correctly in both cases, should we say that the same level of potential development is manifested? If we do not elaborate Vygotsky's insightful but cryptic account of the zone of proximal development, the answer would have to be yes. After all, both children have performed at the same level of potential development as determined through problem solving under adult guidance. But, something seems very wrong about this answer. Some readers might object by pointing out that the nature of the adult's assistance is quite different in the two cases. Such an objection is certainly valid, but it does not go far enough. In order to formulate our objections clearly and thus to understand the mechanics of the zone of proximal development, we must introduce a few additional theoretical constructs. Three notions that I shall outline in this connection are situation definition, intersubjectivity, and semiotic mediation.

The notion of situation definition lays the groundwork for my critique and extension of Vygotsky's ideas, in that all the remaining points I shall make derive from it in one way or another. A situation definition is the way in which a setting or context is represented — that is, defined — by those who are operating in that setting. I use the term *definition* because I want to emphasize that humans actively create a representation of a situation; they are not the passive recipients of this representation. The notion of situation definition is needed in any complete account of the zone of proximal development, because collaboration in this zone typically involves the adult's representing objects and events in one way and the child's representing them in another. This was clearly the case in the earlier hypothetical example of an adult and child doing long division. In such cases, it is misleading to speak of the task setting as if it can be represented in only one way. Rather, it is essential to recognize that, even though the adult and child are functioning in the same spatiotemporal context, they often understand this context in such different ways that they are not really doing the same task. This point has been made at a more general level by Newman and others (in press).

In order to clarify this point about differences in the ways in which an adult and a child define a situation, consider a second, more detailed example. Suppose that an investigator assigns an adult-child dyad the task of constructing one object (the "copy") in accordance with another (the "model"). In this task, there are several possible ways of arranging the pieces so that they make up a copy object, but the only correct solution requires that they be assembled in accordance with the model. When confronted with such a task, preschool children often select a piece without consulting the model to determine whether the piece is needed or where it should go. This does not indicate that these children are acting randomly or that the piece is not represented as part of a coherent situation definition. Rather, it usually reflects the fact that they have defined the task differently than an adult would. Specifically, they usually have defined the setting as one in which they are to use pieces to construct an object without regard to the model. (Note the difficulties in even identifying the objects in this setting without presupposing some situation definition. To refer to something as a copy presupposes the existence of a model and vice versa.)

In studies of adult-child interaction in such a task setting (for example, McLane, 1981; Wertsch, 1979; Wertsch and others, in press) we have seen several instances of a child's constructing the entire copy object without consulting the model. Sometimes the adult allows the child to complete the copy without regard to the model and then finally intervenes to point out the need to reconstruct the copy in accordance with the model, as specified in the original task instructions. In such cases, the child's initial efforts are based on a representation of the pieces that does not take the model into consideration. One might say that each piece is represented as an "object-to-be-used-as-I-see-fit." In contrast, the adult understands each piece in the copy as having a corresponding item in the model. For the adult, the representation is something like "object-to-be-used-in-the-copy-because-of-the-presence-of-a-corresponding-piece-in-the-model."

This brief account of this task setting illustrates the point that one and the same object can be represented or defined in quite different ways. In a very important sense, two different sets of objects are involved in the two cases. Hence, we see that one essential aspect of a situation definition in such task settings is the representation of objects.

So far, I have dealt with object representation as if it can be separated from the action patterns found in a task setting. In fact, this is not so. Indeed, from our illustration it is already clear that differences in object definition or representation are inextricably tied to differences in what someone is doing with the objects. This points to the need to incorporate such a notion as action pattern into an account of situation definition. For the empirical researcher concerned with the zone of proximal development, this means that some sort of explicit account of the action pattern is required. Such an account can be provided by what is frequently called a task analysis (Resnick and Glaser, 1976). In contrast to most studies involving a task analysis, however, studies of interpsychological functioning in the zone of proximal development require at least two task analyses. These analyses correspond to the separate individuals' definitions of the situation. While the child's situation definition corresponds to the actual level in the zone of proximal development, the adult's situation definition does not necessarily correspond to the potential level. This is so because the adult and child can collaborate on the basis of a third situation definition that does not correspond to the adult's representation of the situation. This is a point to which I shall return when examining intersubjectivity and the processes of social interaction in the zone of proximal development.

The required task analyses can be provided by listing the steps involved in a strategic, goal-directed action (Leont'ev, 1981). In the task of constructing a copy object in accordance with a model, the list of strategic steps might be represented as in Action Pattern 1:

Action Pattern 1

Step 1: Consult the model to determine the identity and location of the piece needed next.
Step 2: Select the piece identified in Step 1 from the pieces pile.
Step 3: Add the piece selected in Step 2 to the copy object in accordance with its location in the model.

This account of strategic steps specifies the steps required for the correct identification, selection, and placement of a piece in the copy.

It is important to note here that the notion of correct identification, selection, and placement presupposes the adult's situation definition. That is, it reflects the adult's idea of what action pattern is to be executed. However, the adult's representation of the task setting often does not correspond to the child's. Specifically, the child in our earlier illustration represented task objects in such a way that the model was not taken into account. The action pattern that corresponds to this understanding of objects can be represented as follows:

Action Pattern 2

Step A: Select a piece from the pieces pile.
Step B: Add the piece selected in Step A to the copy.

Such a task analysis includes no mention of the model. As far as the child who follows this action pattern is concerned, no model exists.

An essential point about these action patterns is that the three strategic steps that comprise the first action pattern cannot be derived simply by supplementing the two steps in the second action pattern. By comparing Step 2 in Action Pattern 1 (Select the piece identified in Step 1 from the pieces pile) with Step A in Action Pattern 2 (Select a piece from the pieces pile), we can see why. The same behavior corresponds to both steps, namely, picking up a piece from the pieces pile. However, the functional significance of this behavior is quite different in the two action patterns. When it instantiates Step 2 in Action Pattern 1, the fact that Step 1 is presupposed means that the piece is defined as corresponding to something in the model. Hence, the significance of the piece itself and the reason for picking it up are determined by Step 1. When the behavior of picking up the piece instantiates Step A in Action Pattern 2, no presuppositions about a model are involved. Hence, the representation of the object and the reason for picking it up are quite different than they are when the behavior instantiates Step 2.

This fact has important implications for any account of the developmental transition involved in moving from Action Pattern 2 to Action Pattern 1. It means that this developmental transition cannot be conceptualized in terms of quantitative change; a child cannot simply add another step to an existing action pattern to move to a more adultlike situation definition in this case. Rather, a qualitative transformation is involved. The child must fundamentally redefine his or her definition of the situation in order to make this transition. In an important sense, completely different objects and actions are involved at different levels of development.

I would argue that this process of giving up an existing situation definition in favor of a qualitatively new one is characteristic of the major changes that a child undergoes in the zone of proximal development. Rather than thinking of change in this zone as a steady accretion of knowledge about a task, it is essential to understand that major portions of this change occur through a shift in one's basic understanding of what the objects and events in a setting are. It is perhaps best to think of such change in terms of the sudden insight experience examined by Gestalt psychologists, such as Duncker (1945).

Thus, in order to understand the way in which an individual defines a situation, we have seen that two interrelated issues are involved: the representation of objects and the representation of action patterns for operating on those objects. Furthermore, we have seen that a defining property of the zone of proximal development is that the participants involved in collaborative problem solving have different situation definitions. Finally, we have seen that we cannot account for growth in the zone of proximal development solely in terms of quantitative increments to an existing situation definition. Rather, we must recognize that a fundamental characteristic of such growth is what one might term *situation redefinition* — something that involves giving up a previous situation definition in favor of a qualitatively new one.

Up to this point, I have focused on how separate individuals define a situation. When considering the potential level in the zone of proximal development, however, it is important to remember that it necessarily involves social interaction or functioning on what Vygotsky (1981) termed the *interpsychological plane*. This reflects the claim made in the Editors' Notes of this volume that the zone of proximal development is an instantiation of Vygotsky's general genetic law of cultural development. His emphasis on the interpsychological origins of intrapsychological functioning means that the potential level in the zone of proximal development cannot be conceptualized, let alone measured, solely in terms of an individual's ability. This is the force of Vygotsky's dictum that "instruction *creates* a zone of proximal development" (1956, p. 450; emphasis added). This dictum points to the fact that, even though it is possible to characterize an individual in terms of his or her potential to enter into a certain level of interpsychological functioning, this potential guarantees almost nothing about the level of interpsychological functioning that will actually come into existence in instructional interaction. For this reason, the notion of situation definition must be expanded so that it applies to interpsychological as well as to intrapsychological functioning. This, however, requires the introduction to an additional theoretical construct: intersubjectivity.

For our purposes, we can say that intersubjectivity exists between two interlocutors in a task setting when they share the same situation definition and know that they share the same situation definition. At first glance, it may seem inconsistent to speak of intersubjectivity between an adult and child in the zone of proximal development. After all, I have repeatedly emphasized that interpsychological functioning in this zone is characterized by the fact that the interlocutors have different individual (that is, intrapsychological) situation definitions. In order to deal with this seeming paradox, we need to recognize that intersubjectivity can exist at several different levels. At one extreme, it can consist of no more than agreement on the location of concrete objects in a communication setting. At the other extreme, nearly complete intersubjectivity exists when two interlocutors represent objects and events in identical ways. If this were to happen in adult-child interaction, there would be no reason for the adult to provide any further assistance. The child's actual level of development would already be equivalent to the adult's intrapsychological situation definition and to the potential level that could be attained in interpsychological functioning.

negotiation has been a topic of interest for several investigators during the past decade or so (for example, Gumperz, 1976; Rommetveit, 1974, 1979). A special variant of this process typically occurs in adult-child interpsychological functioning in the zone of proximal development. In the kind of interaction that Vygotsky had in mind, an adult is typically called on to communicate on the basis of a situation definition which differs from the one that he or she would accept independently as most appropriate in the setting. In such cases, several situation definitions can be involved. I have already outlined two of these — the adult's and the child's intrapsychological situation definitions. Adult-child collaboration at the potential level of development often involves yet a third. This third situation definition represents objects and events in a way that will allow communication between the adult and child. In some cases, it corresponds to the child's actual level of development. That is, the dyad can attain intersubjectivity on the basis of the child's intrapsychological situation definition. However, this is not always the case. In many instances, the negotiated intersubjective situation definition that defines the potential level of development is often one that requires the child to change his or her understanding of objects and events. This change can involve the child's shifting to the adult's situation definition, or it can involve a shift to a viewpoint somewhere between the adult's and the child's original intrapsychological situation definitions.

Hence, the adult and child can negotiate an intersubjective situation definition that differs from both of their ways of understanding the situation on the intrapsychological plane. It is essential to recognize an important asymmetry in this type of negotiation, however. This asymmetry derives from the fact that the adult's willingness to accept a second situation definition temporarily by no means indicates a shift in his or her opinion of how the objects and events in the task setting are most appropriately understood or represented. It simply indicates the adult's willingness to do what is necessary to carry out the communicative task at hand. In an important sense, the adult continues to represent the objects and events in a way that is appropriate for mature members of the culture. The only genuine, lasting situation redefinition that takes place occurs on the part of the child.

In order to specify how the negotiation of an intersubjective situation definition occurs, it is important to specify the concrete mechanism that makes it possible. This involves the introduction of the third notion that I see as necessary to the clarification of Vygotsky's account of the zone of proximal development: semiotic mediation. As I have argued elsewhere (Wertsch, 1983, in press, in preparation), Vygotsky's account of mediation by signs, especially linguistic signs, plays a fundamental role in his overall theoretical approach. The phenomena of intersubjectivity and its negotiation are no exceptions. The processes involved in these phenomena are sometimes conceptualized as operating independently of speech, a view that mistakenly assumes that speech simply names or reflects a previously existing situation definition. Such a view overlooks the fact that intersubjectivity is often created through the use of language. In order to clarify this point, consider once again the case of an adult-child dyad in a model-copy task where the adult understands the task in terms of Action Pattern 1 and the child understands it in terms of Action Pattern 2. Even though quite different intrapsychological situation definitions are involved, intersubjectivity can be established if appropriate forms of semiotic mediation are used in communication. Such communication could consist of the adult's directing the child to select and place pieces in locations in the copy without requiring the child to recognize that the pieces and locations correspond to something in the model. Directives such as (1) can serve this purpose very well:

(1) Pick up that red one and put it next to the blue one.

A child can respond appropriately to such directives simply by understanding nonverbal pointing and color terms: He or she is not required to understand that the objects and the actions carried out on these objects have anything to do with the model. The issue here is what the child is required to understand in order to respond appropriately to a directive, not what he or she actually understands. Hence, a child may in fact understand the significance of the model, but in the case of directive 1 this is not required. This illustration shows how a particular way of talking about the objects and events in a setting automatically sets the level at which intersubjectivity is to be established. It is in this sense that speech can create, rather than merely reflect, an intersubjective situation definition.

Before going on to consider how other utterances can create different levels of intersubjectivity, some comments on the examples that I am using are in order. First, the fact that an adult makes an utterance does not guarantee that intersubjectivity will be established at a particular level. The utterance is only a bid in the negotiations. The child must respond appropriately or at least understand the utterance for an intersubjective situation definition to come into existence. Second, the examples that I use focus only on how an adult can use speech to create intersubjectivity. It must be remembered that the child also can make bids in the negotiations. Depending on various developmental and sociocultural factors, the child can play a central role in negotiating new levels of intersubjectivity (see the chapter by Rogoff, Malkin, and Gilbride in this volume). This statement does not conflict with my earlier statement about the asymmetry involved in determining what will ultimately and permanently be accepted by the adult and child as an intrapsychological situation definition; it concerns only the negotiation of a temporary, intersubjective situation definition. I make no attempt here to cover all aspects of bilateral negotiation between adult and child. Rather, my concern is with the prior issue of how intersubjectivity can be created in general through semiotic mediation.

With these qualifications in mind, let us return to our example in order to examine some other possible negotiating moves. For example, instead of uttering directive 1, the adult could use directive 2:

(2) Show me what you need next.

For a child who is operating on the basis of Action Pattern 2, what is needed next is determined solely on the basis of the copy and the pieces pile. Thus, an object may "come next" because it lies beside the last object taken from the pile. In contrast, for the adult it is only by consulting the model that one can determine what comes next. This reflects Action Pattern 1, which lies at the core of the adult's situation definition.

If the child responds to directive 2 on the basis of a different situation definition from the one assumed by the adult, the adult may detect the difference in presuppositions and change his or her negotiating strategy. One way of doing so is to try to establish intersubjectivity on the child's grounds by shifting to a directive like directive 1. Another way of doing so is to use other directives, such as directive 3, in an attempt to help the child unpack the assumptions about object representations and action patterns that the adult's communicative moves presuppose:

(3) Look at this other one and you can tell.

When directive 3 is used as a follow-up directive to 2, it constitutes an attempt to continue operating on the basis of a situation definition that takes the model into consideration. It indicates a type of semiotic flexibility on the part of the adult but a flexibility that differs from simply switching back to intersubjectivity based on the child's intrapsychological situation definition. Instead, it reflects an attempt to reestablish intersubjectivity while simultaneously encouraging the child to participate in all aspects of the three-step action pattern. Of course, this can confuse the child, and the adult may have to return to trying to establish intersubjectivity on the basis of Action Pattern 2 and the associated object representations.

From the perspective of establishing and maintaining smooth functioning on the interpsychological plane, it would seem to be counterproductive for adults to reintroduce their own situation definition after testing the waters and ascertaining that the child represents objects and events differently. Why, then, do adults often do this? There seem to be two reasons. First, using a directive like directive 3 is always tempting for the adult, since it reflects his or her understanding of what the objects and events really are. When communicating with children in a task setting such as the one illustrated here, there is a constant tension between the various situation definitions understood by the adult. As a result, he or she may occasionally slip into communicating on the basis of his or her normal understanding of what the objects and events are, even if the child does not share this understanding. Second, an adult can use a directive like 3 much more purposefully. It can be an invitation to the child to redefine the situation on the adult's terms. By representing objects and events in speech in a certain way, the adult can be attempting to negotiate a new level of intersubjectivity. Thus, an utterance like 3 can serve as an impetus for change in the child's understanding of the situation.

To summarize, I have argued that several conceptual issues must be clarified if we are to understand and utilize Vygotsky's insightful but somewhat cryptic claims about the zone of proximal development. The fundamental theoretical construct that is needed in this connection is that of situation definition. Once we recognize the importance of the fact that one and the same setting can be represented or defined in several different ways, we can proceed in a more concrete way on other issues. Specifically, we need to use such notions as object representation and action pattern to analyze situation definitions. We also need to recognize that in the zone of proximal development more than one situation definition is involved. These points lead then to the issues of intersubjectivity and the negotiation of intersubjectivity through semiotic mediation.

Of course, it is not necessary for investigators to use the specific notions, let alone the terms, that I have proposed here. However, some generally accepted set of theoretical constructs needs to be developed if we are to avoid confusion in conceptualization and communication. We need to know where we stand on such issues as situation definition, intersubjectivity, and semiotic mediation. I have focused on these theoretical constructs because they seem to be points over which confusion is most likely to arise. Furthermore, they are issues that are either presupposed or explicitly involved in much of the existing research on the zone of proximal development.

As examples of how these notions are used in existing research on the zone of proximal development, consider the line of argument followed in some of the other chapters in this volume. In their account of the zone of proximal development in adult-infant interaction, Rogoff, Malkin, and Gilbride deal with the origins of some of the phenomena that I have tried to define. In this connection, their treatment of joint attention is particularly interesting. These authors outline mechanisms of joint attention, such as joint eye gaze, that are manifest in adults' interaction with infants as young as four months of age. Such mechanisms help to lay the groundwork for children's participation in subsequent zones of proximal development. Specifically, they are important in the formation of intersubjectivity. In this regard, it is interesting that these authors take note of the subtle negotiations involved. The situation definitions that are shared in such interpsychological functioning are quite primitive — they involve little more than agreement on the existence and identity of relatively undefined, uncategorized objects. However, without such agreement, any further development of object representation, action pattern, and inter-subjectivity would be impossible.

Further opportunities for applying the theoretical constructs that I have proposed can be found in the chapter by Saxe, Gearhart, and Guberman. These authors begin by pointing out that an account of interaction in the zone of proximal development must recognize the difference between an adult's and a child's understanding of the goal structure involved. The notion of goal structure deals with the general issues that fall under the headings of situation definition, object representation, and action pattern. Some of the most interesting and impressive findings reported by these authors concern semiotic flexibility, as adults adjust their directives in response to the difficulty of the task and the child's ability level. By using a task analysis concerned with goal structure and a semiotic analysis concerned with subordinate directives, these authors are able to identify various patterns of semiotic flexibility on the part of adults. For example, adults shift directives as a function of whether a child had just acted appropriately or inappropriately in the task setting. These shifts reflect the adults' flexibility in using speech to create a new level of intersubjectivity based on the feedback that they receive about the child's intrapsychological situation definition.

These observations about the findings of Rogoff, Malkin, and Gilbride and of Saxe, Gearhart, and Guberman could be extended to a great deal of the other research on the zone of proximal development. The general point is that as we conduct such research we must constantly strive to locate our ideas and findings on a conceptual map of precisely defined theoretical constructs.

References

Brown, A. L., and Ferrara, R. A. "Diagnosing Zones of Proximal Development." In J. V. Wertsch (Ed.), *Culture, Communication, and Cognition: Vygotskian Perspectives.* New York: Cambridge University Press, in press.

Duncker, K. "On Problem Solving." *Psychological Monographs,* 1945, *58* (270) (entire issue).

Gumperz, J. J. "Language, Communication, and Public Negotiation." In P. R. Sanday (Ed.), *Anthropology and the Public Interest.* New York: Academic Press, 1976.

Leont'ev, A. N. "The Problem of Activity in Psychology." In J. V. Wertsch (Ed.), *The Concept of Activity in Soviet Psychology.* Armonk, N.Y.: Sharpe, 1981.

McLane, J. B. "Dyadic Problem Solving: A Comparison of Child-Child and Mother-Child Interaction." Unpublished doctoral dissertation, Northwestern University, 1981.

Newman, D., Griffin, P., and Cole, M. "Laboratory and Classroom Tasks: Social Constraints and the Evaluation of Children's Performance." In B. Rogoff and J. Lave (Eds.), *Everyday Cognition: Its Development in Social Context.* Cambridge, Mass.: Harvard University Press, in press.

Resnick, L. B., and Glaser, R. "Problem Solving and Intelligence." In L. B. Resnick (Ed.), *The Nature of Intelligence.* Hillsdale, N.J.: Erlbaum, 1976.

Rogoff, B., and Gardner, W. "Adult Guidance of Cognitive Development." In B. Rogoff and J. Lave (Eds.), *Everyday Cognition: Its Development in Social Context.* Cambridge, Mass.: Harvard University Press, in press.

Rommetveit, R. *On Message Structure: A Framework for the Study of Language and Communication.* London: Wiley, 1974.

Rommetveit, R. "On the Architecture of Intersubjectivity." In R. Rommetveit and R. Blaker (Eds.), *Studies of Language, Thought, and Verbal Communication.* London: Academic Press, 1979.

Vygotsky, L. S. *Mind in Society: The Development of Higher Psychological Processes.* Cambridge, Mass.: Harvard University Press, 1978.

Vygotsky, L. S. "The Genesis of Higher Mental Functions." In J. V. Wertsch (Ed.), *The Concept of Activity in Soviet Psychology.* Armonk, N.Y.: Sharpe, 1981.

Vygotsky, L. S. *Selected Psychological Investigations.* Moscow, Izdstel'sto Pedagogicheskikh Nauk SSSR, 1956.

Wertsch, J. V. "From Social Interaction to Higher Psychological Processes: A Clarification and Application of Vygotsky's Theory." *Human Development,* 1979, *22,* 1–22.

Wertsch, J. V. "The Role of Semiosis in L. S. Vygotsky's Theory of Human Cognition." In B. Bain (Ed.), *The Sociogenesis of Language and Human Conduct.* New York: Plenum, 1983.

Wertsch, J. V. "The Semiotic Mediation of Mental Life: L. S. Vygotsky and M. M. Bakhtin." In E. Mertz and R. J. Parmentier (Eds.), *Semiotic Mediation: Psychological and Sociocultural Perspectives.* New York: Academic Press, in press.

Wertsch, J. V. *Cognitive Developmental Theory: A Vygotskian Perspective.* In preparation.

Wertsch, J. V., McNamee, G. D., McLane, J. B., and Budwig, N. A. "The Adult-Child Dyad as a Problem-Solving System." *Child Development,* 1980, *51,* 1215–1221.

Wertsch, J. V., Minick, N., and Arns, F. J. "The Creation of Context in Joint Problem Solving: A Cross-Cultural Study." In B. Rogoff and J. Lave (Eds.), *Everyday Cognition: Its Development in Social Context.* Cambridge, Mass.: Harvard University Press, in press.

James V. Wertsch is associate professor and chair, Department of Linguistics, Northwestern University, and research fellow at the Center for Psychosocial Studies.

Our number system is a legacy of our culture. The study of how mothers teach their children about number provides important insights into the way in which children come to interweave their own developing understandings with achievements that have occurred in our culture's social history.

The Social Organization of Early Number Development

Geoffrey B. Saxe
Maryl Gearhart
Steven R. Guberman

Research in cognitive development is generally motivated by the concern to understand the nature of developmental shifts in children's conceptual understandings and logical operations. To pursue this research interest, investigators have often studied children removed from the everyday social contexts in which they use their conceptual skills, and they have interviewed and observed children as they solved problems without the support and collaboration of others. While divorcing the investigation of children's conceptual development from the social contexts in which it occurs permits the researcher greater access to the child's reasoning processes, it removes from observation the ways in which the development of children's reasoning is supported and informed by interactions with others.

The writings of Vygotsky (1962, 1978) and recent elaborations of his works (for example, Wertsch, 1979) address the social network of meanings, activities and historical achievements within which the individual operates and

This research was supported by grants from the National Institute of Education (NIE-G-80-0119), the Spencer Foundation, and the Research Committee of UCLA (No. #3862).

B. Rogoff, J. V. Wertsch (Eds.). *Children's Learning in the "Zone of Proximal Development."*
New Directions for Child Development, no. 23. San Francisco: Jossey-Bass, March 1984.

learns. Using such constructs as the zone of proximal development, Vygotsky argues that an analysis of the social organization of a child's problem-solving efforts is essential to an understanding of cognitive development and its cultural origins. Vygotsky's approach has provided us with a framework for investigating the social roots of one domain of cognitive development, children's numerical cognition.

The development of number is a particularly fruitful domain for the investigation of developmental relations between culture and cognition. Number systems are evolving cultural constructions. This is apparent both in the wide cultural diversity of number systems (Saxe and Posner, 1982) and in the remarkable history of our own number system and procedures for calculation (Menninger, 1969). In focusing on aspects of the social organization of children's early number development, we gain access to a process whereby an evolving cultural construction—the number system—is communicated to children and children transform and incorporate that construction into the fabric of their own cognitive activities. In our research, we have been examining that process by observing how mothers teach their children to solve a counting problem.

Our analysis of adult-child interactions is set within a general model of cognitive development. It is our view that children's novel cognitive constructions result from the dynamic interplay between their elaboration of problem-solving goals and coherent means to achieve those goals. As children identify new goals, they attempt to elaborate novel cognitive means, including conceptual structures, symbolic vehicles, and problem-solving strategies, in order to achieve those goals. These cognitive constructions in turn provide a new framework within which individuals attempt to identify new goals. The aim of our research on mother-child interactions is to explore whether and how mothers participate in the child's elaboration of problem-solving goals and problem-solving means.

Research Plan

In order to study the social organization of goals during mother-child teaching interactions about number, we videotaped mothers and their two-and-one-half- to five-year-old children as the mothers attempted to teach their children a number reproduction game. We also interviewed children individually to obtain a characterization of children's unassisted performances on the number reproduction and other related tasks. For the interaction session, we instructed mothers that the goal of the number reproduction game was to get the same number of pennies (from an available set of fifteen) as there were Cookie Monsters (pictures of the puppet from the "Sesame Street" television show) on the model board, and we encouraged mothers to organize the interaction in whatever way they felt would encourage learning and understanding in their child. We asked the mothers to keep the pennies five to six feet away from the model and to have their children bring the pennies back in a cup.

These instructions were designed to discourage the mothers from organizing local task completion strategies, such as pairing pennies with cookie monsters one by one, strategies that radically simplify the goal of numerical reproduction. Mothers helped their children to complete the task four times for model set sizes of three, four, nine, and ten, in that order. We thus varied task difficulty according to the number of Cookie Monster pictures in the model.

To understand the goal structure that emerges during the adult-child teaching interactions, we found it necessary to develop a method of study in which we produced a coordinated set of analyses of three aspects of the numerical activity. The method entailed an analysis of the goal structure of the activity as it was understood by the mother (or practiced in "culture"), a developmental analysis of the goal structure that children imposed on the activity, and an analysis of how the adult participated in the child's construction of the goals in the activity. In the discussion that follows, we show that each of these analyses is a necessary complement of the others, and we show that together they lead to new insights about how childrens' developing numerical understandings are jointly rooted in their own constructive activities and in their social interactions with others.

Analysis of the Goal Structure
of the Number Reproduction Task

To understand the functional requirements of any task — the work that the subject needs to accomplish in order to solve the task — an analysis of the goal structure that leads to task solution is necessary. The counting game that we asked mothers to teach to their children is similar to many everyday counting activities. To reproduce a given quantity of objects, as our task requires, an individual must accomplish a hierarchy of goals and subgoals. The superordinate goal is to produce an accurate numerical copy. In order to accomplish this, the subject must first accomplish a subgoal: produce an accurate estimate of the model. One means of accomplishing this subgoal is by counting the model. In order to count, further subgoals must be elaborated and accomplished, such as applying the sequence of number words in one-to-one correspondence with the target elements. Once the goals pertaining to the model have been achieved, a similar set of subgoals must be constructed to obtain an accurate number of objects from the available set. Finally, the individual can choose to check his or her accuracy by either recounting the sets or by establishing a one-to-one correspondence between the two sets.

Although the description of the goal structure just presented corresponds to the procedures that we as adults would use to produce a solution to the numerical reproduction task, it does not correspond to the organization of the child's activity as he or she proceeds to solve the task. In order to understand how adults can influence and elaborate children's goals, it is first necessary to understand children's goals during their solution of the task.

A Developmental Analysis of Children's Goals

An analysis of children's unassisted performances on the numerical reproduction task reveals that younger children do not simply make errors in their solution of the task but that they conceptualize the task quite differently than adults do. Table 1 contains a summary description of developmental shifts in children's unassisted performance on numerical reproduction tasks and what we infer to be general features of children's goals associated with these behaviors (see Saxe 1977, 1979).

Young children (Level 1) who are presented with the task often act as if they have two distinct and fluctuating goals during this activity. One goal is to get some or all the elements in the available set. If, during their activity, these children are asked whether counting the model would help them, some (Level 1A) seem to construct another goal: to produce a count of one set or of both sets continuously as if they were one. Slightly more advanced children (Level 1B) focus on producing separate counts of the sets but do not use the information obtained to relate the copy to the model. It is important to note that when children at Levels 1A or 1B identify counting as a goal of the activity, they seem to do so only with regard to the production of a count of a single array. Thus, if they produce two counts (Level 1B), they treat their counts separately, and they do not compare the values that they produce. Moreover, children at these levels often do not treat the last number word of their count as having a cardinal value. For instance, if a child at either sublevel counts a set and is then asked how many items there are in the set, the child is likely either to recount the set or to offer the last several number words of the count as a reply.

At Level 2, children's goals seem to shift. Now, children exhibit double array goals: They produce separate and distinct numerical representations of the model and copy, which they compare. Nonetheless, their solution strategy at Level 2A remains different from that of adults. Children at Level 2A count the model and available set without a clearly articulated overall plan for the

Table 1. Developmental Analysis of Children's Goals on Numerical Reproduction Task

Level	Child's Behavior	Inferred Goals
1A	Child brings all of available set. "Would counting help?" Child counts only own copy.	Single array goals
1B	Same as 1A, but child counts model and copy and produces no subsequent modifications.	Single array goals
2A	Child equalizes model and copy through successive counts, additions, and subtractions.	Double array goals
2B	Systematic reproduction using counting.	Double array goals

task. Then, through a process of recounts and successive additions and subtractions, they attempt to equalize the model and their copy. At Level 2B, children produce systematic counts and an accurate reproduction of the model.

A Framework for Understanding the Emergent Goal Structure of the Activity During Mother-Child Interaction

The actual goal structure of the activity as it emerged over the course of mother-child interactions was analyzed by constructing coding schemes that were guided both by a logical analysis of the goal structure of the number reproduction activity as communicated to the mothers and by developmental analysis of the child's shifting goals.

We suspected that adults interweave their instruction with children's ongoing problem-solving activities by adjusting the goal structure of tasks to children's level of functioning. For instance, in presenting the number reproduction task to children, mothers can define or help their children to accomplish goals at any one of many levels of task structure. Table 2 contains the hierarchical description of the goals and subgoals of the task. Mothers can offer directives during the interaction at any of these levels.

At the most general goal structure levels, the mother presents the goal structure of the entire task without specifying any of the subgoals (directives 1 and 2). At each of these levels of description, the mother provides a double array goal — the child must produce and compare numerical representations of the model and the copy. At the next level (directive 3), the mother guides the child to a specific subgoal by directing the child to get a specific number of pennies from the available set. This form of directive is transitional between a double array and a single array goal specification of the task in that the mother directs her child to produce a specific representation of the available set of pennies (single array goal), but she does so in the context of achieving a representation of the model set. The remaining directives entail increasing specificity of how to achieve a numerical representation of the model set, each referring to a single array goal or to some aspect of a single array goal. For instance, at the fourth level, the mother asks the child for a numerical representation of the model without providing information on how to accomplish this. At the fifth level, the mother specifies not only the subgoal concerning the need for a representation but also the further subgoal concerning the need to count to achieve the representation. The remaining levels each represent more specific directives concerning how to achieve an accurate count.

Analyses of the Interactions

On the basis of the children's unassisted performances, we divided them into two groups, a low-ability group and a high-ability group. We inferred that these groups would tend to apply single and double array goals respectively to

Table 2. A Hierarchical Ordering of Maternal Directives
for the Numerical Reproduction Task

Maternal Directive	Example
Directives Pertaining to the Goal Structure of the Entire Task	
1. Mother provides the superordinate goal of the entire task.	"Get just the same number of pennies as Cookie Monsters."
2. Mother provides the superordinate goal of the entire task after a representation of the model has been accomplished.	"Get just the same number of pennies as Cookie Monsters."
Directives Linking a Representation of the Model with a Production of a Copy	
3. Mother directs the child to obtain a specified number from the available set.	"Go get nine pennies for the Cookie Monsters."
Directives to Produce a Representation of the Model	
4. Mother directs child to produce a representation of the model without specifying how to do so.	"How many Cookie Monsters are there?"
5. Mother directs child to produce a representation of the model and specifies a procedure whereby this can be accomplished.	"Count the Cookie Monsters."
6–10. Mother provides increasing assistance on some aspect of the child's counting activity with each successive level.	Mother counts as child points to each Cookie Monster.
Directives Providing a Representation of the Model	
11. Mother provides a cardinal representation of the model for the child.	"There are three Cookie Monsters."

the reproduction tasks during the interactions. We then conducted a number of analyses on the interactions using the scheme presented in Table 2 to determine whether and in what way mothers adjusted the organization of the task to the child's understanding of the task's goal structure.

Task Introductions. First, we asked whether mothers introduced the task differently to children of different ability levels of numerical competence. For this analysis, we examined introductions only to set sizes three and nine, since many mothers organized set sizes four and ten as problems of addition to set sizes three and nine, not as independent trials.

We found that mothers were making adjustments appropriate to the ability levels of their child. The mothers of low-ability children introduced the task differently from the mothers of high-ability children. Most mothers of low-ability children began with a single array subgoal request (for example, a Level 4 "How many Cookie Monsters are there?" or a Level 5 "Count the

Cookie Monsters"). A few mothers of low-ability children formulated a super-ordinate double array goal, but they used it only as a context for a more specific single array subgoal request. Here is an example of such a strategy:

Example 1. Low-Ability Child; Set Size: 3

Mother: Are you ready to learn a game? (Mother leans over to look in child's face. Mother gives cup to child.) Okay [What] we're going to do is we're going to count the Cookie Monsters. Okay? (Mother pushes set size three Cookie Monster boards towards child while pointing to each monster.) And, then I want you to go over to the pile of pennies over there and put the same number of pennies in the cup. . . so all the Cookie Monsters have one. (Superordinate as Context)

Child: Okay.

Mother: Okay? So, should we count the Cookie Monsters? (Level 5 directive)

A few mothers of low-ability subjects immediately transformed the entire goal structure of the task and presented a simplified goal structure (not coded within the levels analysis); for example, "I want you to get a cookie [a penny] and put it in the cup to give it to the Cookie Monster." Such a simplification redefined the task from a numerical one to one that involved non-numerical correspondences. Thus, the task structure presented to these children was neither one that entailed double nor single array goals. Instead, the goal merely entailed getting elements of a set. We find these adjustments all the more significant in light of our attempts to prevent such radical simplifications in our initial instructions to the mothers.

No mother of a high-ability child ever immediately simplified the goal structure of the task, nor did any of these mothers specify the means for achieving a representation of the model, that is, counting (Level 5). The typical introduction for mothers of high-ability children was, "How many Cookie Monsters are there?" (Level 4), a request intended to help focus the child on the need to achieve a numerical representation of a single array (the model set of Cookie Monsters) without specifying the means for doing so. Some mothers of high-ability children specified just the superordinate goal (for example, "You have to get the same number of pennies as there are Cookie Monsters and put them in the cup" [Level 1]). In contrast, mothers of low-ability children never specified just a superordinate goal.

Mothers tended to introduce set size nine numerical reproductions differently from set size three. Some mothers in both high- and low-ability groups adapted their task introductions to set size nine by increasing their assistance and initiating the task with a more subordinate directive. In addition, we found another form of adaptation for the mothers of high-ability children. The trial for set size nine was always preceded by trials for set sizes three and four. Some of the mothers of high-ability children made use of these previous interactions by introducing the task with a request that the child merely

"Do this one now"—an "empty" task marker that displayed the mother's belief that after two trials her child now shared with her an understanding of the task goals. No mother of a low-ability child ever introduced the task with only a marker of this nature.

Formulations of Superordinate Goals. The preceding analysis indicates that mothers of high-ability and low-ability children differed in the degree to which they specified the task structure in their introductions. Mothers of low-ability children tended to structure the subgoals for their children to a much greater extent than did mothers of high-ability children. In a related analysis, we examined whether mothers ever formulated the superordinate goal of numerical reproduction (Level 1 or Level 2 in Table 2) at any point in the model phase (when the child was to determine the number of Cookie Monsters) or in the initiation of the available set phase (when the child went to get the same number of pennies).

In set size three, most mothers of both low-ability and high-ability children formulated the superordinate task goal at some point before the child gathered pennies from the available set. In set size nine, however, most mothers of low-ability subjects did not formulate the superordinate goal, while most mothers of high-ability subjects were still likely to formulate the superordinate goal. It is likely that, by set size nine, the mothers of low-ability subjects had learned from repeated task trials that the superordinate double array goal was not understood by their children and thus that formulation of it was not useful in supporting their child's task activity.

Median Assistance Levels. In order to obtain an index of the extent to which the mothers themselves structured the subgoals of the task for their children, we next calculated a median score for each mother's goal directives in the model phase for each set size. Consistent with the analyses of task introductions and superordinate goal formulations, we found that mothers of high-ability children gave their children less assistance in constructing the subgoals of the task than did mothers of low-ability children. We also found that task complexity influenced the teaching strategies of mothers of both high-ability and low-ability children. As task complexity increased, both groups of mothers shifted to more subordinate goal directives. Examples 2 and 3 illustrate the way in which the mother of a high-ability child adjusts the goal structure of the task as a function of the model's set size. In this case, the adjustment occurs in the task introduction.

Example 2. High-Ability Child; Set Size 3; Median Assistance: 3.0

Mother: Look at this board. Now, can you tell me how many Cookie Monsters are on there? (Level 4 directive)

Child: Yep. One, two, three. (Child touches each Cookie Monster.)

Mother: Okay. Now, the trick is this. We have to—you have to get the same amount of pennies and put them in the cup that are on here. (Mother points to cup and touches board. Child goes to penny pile.) (Level 2 directive)

Example 3. High-Ability Child; Set Size: 9; Median Assistance: .5

Mother: Close your eyes. (Mother gets set size nine board. Child opens eyes and gasps.) Wow! Now, can you count? (Level 5 directive)

Child: One, two, three, four, five, six, seven, eight, nine. (Child touches each Cookie Monster in turn.)

Mother: Okay. How many Cookie Monsters are there? (Uptake on last numeral)

Child: Nine. (Child "sings," sweeping hand around board.)

Mother: Now we have to put the same amount in the cup that are here. (Level 2 directive)

Mothers' Shifts in Goal Directives Within Set Size. Not only do mothers adjust their organization of the task as a function of the child's ability level and task difficulty, but the social organization of the task is dynamic and shifts during an interaction as a function of whether the child achieves an accurate count. We found that mothers generally shifted to a goal directive subordinate to their previous one after the child produced an inaccurate count and that mothers generally shifted to a superordinate goal directive after the child produced an accurate count. These trends occurred regardless of task difficulty and the child's ability level. Example 4 illustrates a shift to a subordinate goal following an incorrect count (Level 4 to Level 10 assistance) and a shift to a more superordinate goal following an accurate count (Level 10 to Level 3 assistance).

Example 4. High-Ability Child; Set Size: 9; Median Assistance: 4.0

Mother: Here's one that's much harder. (Mother puts out set size nine board.) How many Cookie Monsters do we have here? (Level 4 directive)

Child: One, two, three, four, five, six, seven, eight, nine, ten. (After two, child points either miss or repeat Cookie Monsters.)

Mother: Let me help you count them, okay? (Mother and child count and point in unison until five, whereupon child mistakenly says seven.) Forgot, you forgot about five. (Mother and child count and point in unison from five to nine.) (Level 10 assistance) Golly, that's a lot. Can you count nine pennies and put them in the cup? (Level 3 directive)

Mothers' Uptake on Children's Accurate Counts. The use of the last number word of the count to represent the quantity in the model array presents special difficulty for children, and the analysis of developmental shifts in this understanding has received considerable attention in the research literature on children's early cognitive development (Gelman and Gallistel, 1978; Gelman and Meck, in press; Schaeffer and others, 1974). To assess how mothers signal the special utility of the last number word, we focused on what mothers said following the child's first accurate count as a function of the child's ability level. For instance, once the child completed a count, some mothers repeated the number word; others asked the child how many there were. We found that mothers of low-ability children provided an uptake on the last number word of the child's count more often than did mothers of high-ability children. In addition, the frequency of mothers' uptakes tended to increase with task difficulty for high-ability children.

Summary and Conclusions

In this chapter, we have provided coordinated analyses of three aspects of the social context of children's developing conceptual understandings: an analysis of children's developing operations within a knowledge domain, a functional analysis of the cultural task context in which these operations are deployed, and an analysis of the way in which other people can bridge and adapt the cultural definition of the task to the child's developing operations. We believe that the insights gained from this type of analytic approach are critical in understanding the way in which young children come to make the historical achievements of culture a part of their own problem-solving activities.

At the beginning of this chapter, we argued that very young children who engage in the number reproduction activity often impose the goal of producing a count of a single array (Levels 1A and 1B) on the nominal task and that their means of accomplishing the count are typically not well developed. The results for our low-ability subjects indicate that their mothers provided assistance appropriate to their developing numerical operations. For instance, these mothers were more likely to initiate the task with specific directives, such as, "Count the Cookie Monsters." Moreover, as the greater median assistance levels reveal, these mothers often assisted their children's model set counts by modeling or directing very low-level subgoals, such as the repetition of number words in the correct sequence or the assignment of number words in one-to-one correspondence with objects (Levels 6 through 11). In their uptakes to accurate counts, these mothers also attempted to highlight to their children that the last number word recited could be used as a summary description (cardinal representation) of the entire array. Not surprisingly, these mothers were less likely than the mothers of high-ability children to formulate only the overall double array goal structure of the task, and they were less likely than the mothers of high-ability children ever to formulate it. Thus, the mothers themselves more often took responsibility for relating the numerical value of the model to that of the copy. We interpret these mother-child interactions as a context for the low-ability child to generate a system of understanding and symbolization that is commensurate with the child's definition of the goal structure of the task: the representation of single arrays by means of our conventional numeration system.

Older preschool children begin to construe the task as having a double array goal structure. They attempt to produce numerical representations of the model using the means that they have developed to achieve single array goals. This generally entails counting the model and the available set and then, by a trial-and-error process, equalizing them through a succession of counts, additions and subtractions, and recounts (Level 2A). Gradually, these older children structure increasingly systematic solution strategies so that they organize their counting to achieve a precise copy (Level 2B). The results for high-ability children revealed that mothers provided directives that supported the child's construction of these systematic solution strategies. Mothers of high-ability children were more likely to introduce the task at superordinate goal levels, and they were more likely to formulate the goal structure of the entire task when using large set sizes. These mothers provided less assistance in the model phase, and they were less likely than mothers of low-ability children to provide uptake on the last number word of their children's counts. Thus, they were more likely to relinquish responsibility to the child for relating the numerical value of the model to that of the copy.

In addition to these group differences, we found that all mothers continually adjusted the goal structure of the task during the activity itself. So, while children of low ability succeeded less often than did children of high ability, their mothers, like the mothers of high-ability children, tended to shift to more superordinate goal directives when the children did succeed. Similarly, when children of both ability levels had difficulty, mothers shifted to more subordinate goal levels.

The analyses that we have presented in this chapter indicate that the goal structure of numerical activities as they occur in social interactions is an emergent phenomenon: Located neither in the head of the mother nor in that of the child, this goal structure is negotiated in the interaction itself. Thus, the emergent goal structure simultaneously involves the child's understandings and the historical achievements of culture as communicated by the mother. We argued that children construct means to achieve these socially negotiated goals. For a young child, this can entail the imitation of the number string in the same sequence as the mother articulates it. For an older child, it can entail discovering the importance of systematically counting both the model and the copy. As children generate coherent means to achieve these socially negotiated goals, they create for themselves a system of representation that reflects achievements that have been generated in our culture's social history.

References

Gelman, R., and Gallistel, R. *The Child's Understanding of Number.* Cambridge, Mass.: Harvard University Press, 1978.

Gelman, R., and Meck, E. "Preschoolers' Counting: Principles Before Skill or Skill Before Principles?" *Cognition,* in press.

Menninger, K. *Number Words and Number Symbols.* Cambridge, Mass.: M.I.T. Press, 1969.

Saxe, G. B. "A Developmental Analysis of Notational Counting." *Child Development,* 1977, *48,* 1512–1520.

Saxe, G. B. "Developmental Relations Between Notational Counting and Number Conservation." *Child Development,* 1979, *50,* 180–187.

Saxe, G. B., and Posner, J. "The Development of Numerical Cognition: Cross-Cultural Perspectives." In H. P. Ginsburg (Ed.), *The Development of Mathematical Thinking.* New York: Academic Press, 1982.

Schaeffer, B., Eggleston, V. H., and Scott, J. L. "Number Development in Young Children." *Cognitive Psychology,* 1974, *6,* 357–379.

Vygotsky, L. S. *Thought and Language.* Cambridge, Mass.: M.I.T. Press, 1962.

Vygotsky, L. S. *Mind in Society: The Development of Higher Psychological Processes.* Cambridge, Mass.: Harvard University Press, 1978.

Wertsch, J. V. "From Social Interaction to Higher Psychological Processes: A Clarification and Application of Vygotsky's Theory." *Human Development,* 1979, *22,* 1–22.

The authors are affiliated with the University of California at Los Angeles. Geoffrey B. Saxe is an associate professor in the Graduate School of Education, Maryl Gearhart is a postdoctoral fellow at the Mental Retardation Research Center, and Steven R. Guberman is a doctoral student in the Graduate School of Education.

Young children rapidly develop into socialized participants in their culture through a finely tuned combination of infants' skills and the guidance of more experienced people.

Interaction with Babies as Guidance in Development

Barbara Rogoff
Catherine Malkin
Kathleen Gilbride

Newborn infants are quite ignorant regarding the workings of the society into which they are born. By age three, however, children are socialized participants in their culture. It is the thesis of this chapter that the rapid development of babies into socialized participants in society is accomplished through a finely tuned combination of the infant's skills and the guidance of more experienced people. First, we discuss some characteristics of infants that seem suited for quickly picking up great amounts of information about their new environment. Then, we describe some characteristics of adult-infant interaction that we regard as well adapted to the gradual immersion of infants in the skills and beliefs of the society. (See also Rogoff, in press.) Our argument that infant skills and adult-infant interactional strategies together produce development is

The authors are grateful to Jim Bilagody and Barbara Radziszewski for transcription of videotapes and discussion of ideas and to the adults and babies who participated in the study. A draft of this chapter was presented at the meetings of the Society for Research in Child Development, Detroit, April 1983. The research reported in this chapter was funded by NIH Biomedical Research Support Grant RR7092 to the University of Utah.

B. Rogoff, J. V. Wertsch (Eds.). *Children's Learning in the "Zone of Proximal Development."*
New Directions for Child Development, no. 23. San Francisco: Jossey-Bass, March 1984.

illustrated with data from observations of twenty-six adults interacting with one of two babies during play with a jack-in-a-box.

Children's Role in Their Own Development

Infants come into the world equipped with effective ways of ensuring proximity to more experienced members of society and of becoming involved with their physical and social surroundings. New babies' cries and smiles, for example, successfully elicit attention from adults. The fact that infants become calm when held rewards adults for keeping them near. Rocking and walking are not only effective ways of calming babies but also provide them with adult legs to move on and with access to new scenes of regard that yield information about the environment. With maturation, babies' skills increase so that they are able to hold on to caretakers, to cry when a familiar adult departs, and to approach adults in order to maintain proximity. They explore whatever comes within reach, and one of the caretakers' main jobs is to supervise the babies' access to objects.

Babies use adults as a safe base for exploration; they observe the actions of adults and look to adults for interpretations of unusual events. In this way, infants employ adults as guides for further exploration and learning. During times of uncertainty, one-year-olds actively reference their mothers' emotional expression, turning to the mother and attempting to benefit from her appraisal of the situation (Feinman, 1982; Sorce and others, 1981). If she seems to be interested in and enjoying a situation, the infant ventures out and explores. If the mother shows fear or anger, the infant stops exploring, avoids the situation, or retreats to the mother. Such referencing is facilitated by the ability of one-year-olds to obtain information from the direction in which caregivers point and gaze (Butterworth and Cochran, 1980; Lempers, 1979). Anyone who has functioned alone in a foreign culture can identify with infants' strategies for learning: Stay close to a trusted guide, watch what the guide does and experiences, participate in the guide's activities, and learn from any information that the guide provides.

Children actively involve themselves in situations that allow learning to occur. This is evident in their sometimes obnoxious presence at the scene of activity. Parents often find their toddlers or preschoolers in the way or insisting on "helping" with a task. Parents may be more concerned with getting the dishes clean or the gift wrapped than with instructing children in the principles of soap and water or the geometry of fitting paper around a gift. Childrens' insistence on involvement, however, is likely to be instrumental in gaining a greater understanding of such principles.

We suggest that many of the characteristics of infants and young children place them in a position to seek information about the world around them as that world is construed by their caretakers. They advance their own development by using whatever resources and skills they possess to gain further access to learning experiences through involvement with people, materials, and activities. They are thus active participants in their own development.

Features of Adult-Infant Interaction
That Facilitate Development

Adults facilitate children's learning both by arranging appropriate sequences of materials and tasks for the child and by transmitting information and strategies to the child as they participate together in an activity. Adults provide access to activities, adjust children's participation to an appropriate level, and modify children's responsibility as expertise grows.

Our perspective on adult-child interaction as guidance in development has been influenced by the work of Vygotsky, the Laboratory of Comparative Human Cognition, Wertsch and his colleagues, and Bruner, Wood, and their colleagues. Vygotsky (1962, 1978) emphasized that the social context is instrumental in guiding cognitive development both through the provision of culturally developed tools and practices, such as calculators, writing systems, and event scripts, that facilitate and channel cognitive activities as well as through social interaction with more experienced members of society, in which information regarding tools and practices is transmitted in the zone of proximal development. The more experienced partner engages the child in solving a problem by creating a "scaffolded" (that is, a supported) situation that allows the child to extend current skills and knowledge to a higher level of competence (Vygotsky, 1978; Wertsch, 1979; Wood, 1980).

During communication in the zone of proximal development, the adult assesses the child's current understanding of the material and adjusts the scaffolding to support the child's developing skill. The child simultaneously adjusts the pace of instruction according to his or her needs and guides the adult in constructing the scaffold. Both adult and child are thus actively involved in solving the problem. The adult does not solve the problem while the child passively observes and spontaneously extracts the information. Rather, in the effective use of the zone of proximal development, the adult guides the child through the process of solving the problem, with the child participating at a comfortable but slightly challenging level.

The adult's role in guiding the child's participation in problem solving does not necessarily involve awareness of instructing on the part of the adult. The adult's arrangements for learning often involve tacit and opportunistic use of available resources in a particular problem situation rather than explicit recipes for solution that do not rely on joint participation in the activity. The adult emphasizes crucial actions, provides guidance at choice points, and indicates important alternatives in the solution of the problem at hand. The child's state of understanding and contribution to the activity further tailor the interaction to the specific teaching-learning situation. Information and skills are thus conveyed through the shared construction of the solution rather than through explicit freestanding directions on how to solve the problem.

The tacit nature of instruction may be clearest in infancy, since few adults regard themselves as teaching infants, although they routinely adjust their interaction and structure the environment in ways that provide support for the infant's learning. Researchers in prelinguistic development have noted that adults carry on conversations with their infants in which the baby's role as conversational partner is adjusted to the baby's repertoire (Brown, 1958; Bruner, 1981; Bernstein, 1981; Cazden, 1979; Ochs, 1979). Adults support the baby's participation by providing responses to their own questions, by repeating and expanding on the infant's contributions, and by providing visual supports and redundant information to clarify their own and the infant's meanings and thereby aid the infant's learning. Infants' conversational turns first involve coos and burps, then later involve babbling, and eventually require speaking words. As babies' repertoires increase, adults continually raise the stakes, holding out for the most advanced form of participation from their partners. The structure of adult-child discourse provides scaffolding that allows children to participate in conversations that are beyond their competence in discourse. Such participation may advance children's skills. For example, the pattern of joint adult-child construction of propositions from one-word utterances appears to form the foundation of the child's combinations of words (Scollon, 1976).

The tacit arrangement of learning by adults is also evident in their selection of appropriate tasks and materials for children's current state of understanding, even without face-to-face interaction. Adults play a large role in determining what objects (for example, toys and books) are available, what spectacles (for example, television shows, birth of a sibling) are allowed, what chores children are involved in, what companions are available, and what access children have to observing their parents' work and recreation. Providing access to these activities is instrumental in children's learning, although adults seldom regard this role as instructional.

In addition to providing access to activities and thereby arranging the occurrence of cognitive tasks, adults facilitate children's learning by regulating the difficulty of tasks. To do this, the adult segments tasks into manageable subgoals. This role is apparent in the adult's decisions about what level of activity a child may participate in, even when the adult is not constantly interacting with the child in the performance of the activity. For example, parents regulate the task of learning to cook on the basis of the child's skills, the parent's interest in the child's learning those skills, and pragmatic factors, such as cleanliness or time pressure in preparing breakfast. A child may be allowed to stir the eggs at age two, to break them at age three, to dish them up at age four, and to turn the stove on at age five. Arrangement and simplification of the task assist the child in learning.

The adult's management of subgoals of the task is also apparent in interactional situations, where the level of the adult's involvement is tailored to the child's expertise. With a novice, the adult may take responsibility for managing the subgoals as well as the overall goal of the activity, while with a more experienced child, the adult may give responsibility for subgoals to the child.

Since the child's expertise grows over the course of a single session, the division of responsibility changes during the interaction. Initially, the adult may take responsibility for structuring the task and managing progress toward the goal, but the adult must also assure the appropriate transfer of responsibility to the child for managing the activity. This requires sensitivity to the child's competence in the particular task, which involves a tacit theory of development and task analysis. The transfer of responsibility can be a subtle process involving successive attempts by the participants to assay the novice's readiness for greater responsibility. Over the course of learning, the highly supportive scaffolding is removed interactively so that the child continues to participate at a comfortable yet challenging level.

One way in which the scaffolding can be provided is by making messages redundant, so that if a child does not understand one aspect of the communication other forms are readily available to make the meaning clear. As the child develops greater understanding, the adult and child adjust the level of scaffolding necessary to support the child's learning by reducing the level of redundancy. In early parent-child communication, the adult facilitates the infant's acquisition of language by supporting a verbal message with enough redundant nonverbal information to ensure the infant's understanding (Greenfield, in press). As the infant becomes able to comprehend the verbal message, the adult decreases the amount of nonverbal information.

Adults can test the child's readiness by reducing the level of scaffolding, thereby allowing the child to participate to a greater extent. But if the child indicates lack of understanding, the adult can quickly and subtly re-erect the scaffolding that has momentarily been removed. The adult's assessment of the child's current understanding as well as the adult's adjustment of the scaffold frequently rely on very subtle cues, such as hesitance, direction of gaze, and postural changes, as well as on errors by the child.

It should be emphasized that the social guidance of development is jointly arranged by the participants. Both adult and child are responsible for structuring and pacing the instructional communication and learning activities. They jointly manage the transfer of responsibility for the task. As the child's capabilities develop, the support is adjusted to a level just beyond that which the child can manage independently.

Guided Development as Adults and Babies Play with a Toy

We will use observations of adults' interactions with babies to illustrate our arguments regarding adults' and babies' arrangement of development through their joint responsibility for guided participation in an activity.

Twenty-six adults interacted with one of two babies (twin sister and brother) between the ages of four and seventeen months. The adults were ten men and sixteen women who ranged in age between eighteen and seventy-seven and who varied in their experience with babies. Twelve of the adults were strangers to the babies, five were acquaintances, and nine were relatives. Half of the twenty-six sessions involved the girl baby, and half involved the boy. The ages sampled were four months (four observations), five months (three observations), six months (four observations), seven to eight months (three observations), nine to ten months (four observations), eleven to fourteen months (four observations), and fifteen to seventeen months (four observations). The sessions occurred in the babies' home, with their mother (the first author) present. The adult was asked to try to get the baby to talk and smile and play with toys. The segment of interaction analyzed in this chapter involves play with the jack-in-a-box, one of eleven toys available. About half of the adults spontaneously used the jack-in-a-box, and the other half used it on the mother's suggestion.

The data consist of transcripts describing the sequence of adults' and baby's communicative actions: their vocalizations and intonations, postural changes, gaze, gestures, and actions with objects. The aim of transcription was to analyze maximally the participants' adaptations to each other in the particular task by utilizing context-specific information (for example, the preceding and subsequent actions of both participants) to understand the processes involved (see Rogoff, in press). Transcriptions made independently by two observers viewing the same videotaped segment indicated great congruence in the accounts produced by different observers. It is interesting to note that this congruence did not require extensive training and that observers represented different cultures (Anglo, Navajo, and Polish) and varied in their familiarity with the research topic (undergraduate, graduate student, and faculty member).

In the early months (four to six months), interactions focus on the maintenance of the baby's attention to the adult and the ongoing activity, through subtle negotiations. Both the baby and the adult contribute to the management of joint attention. The baby rewards the adult with eye contact, smiles, and cooperation when the adult successfully meshes the adult's agenda with the baby's interests and is sensitive to the baby's cues. The baby withdraws eye contact when the adult appears to be intrusive, uninvolved, or oblivious to the baby's cues. If the adult continues to miss the baby's cues, the baby escalates — beginning with listlessness, then gaze aversion, then postural distancing, then turning the whole body away and hiding the face in the forearms. Vocal cues begin with whines, grunts, or whimpers, which can become insistent fussing or cries and shrieks. The progression of actions by the baby and the progression of actions by the adult are tied together.

The adult's moves are contingent on the baby's involvement, with attempts to maintain joint attention through eye contact, verbal or nonverbal emphasis of events, and control of access to objects. The adult withdraws access to a toy or discontinues an activity when the baby appears to have lost interest in the adult or the adult's agenda. When the baby shows interest, the adult encourages joint focus of attention by adding emphasis to significant events and by seeking eye contact in order to share the experience. Even with babies as young as four months, adults focused the baby's attention on the sudden emergence of Bugs Bunny from the jack-in-a-box by jumping in mock surprise. They elicited mutual gaze by asking, "Did you see that?" or, "My, what happened?" as confirmation of the joint attention of adult and baby to the sudden event. One adult commented to the baby on the difficulty of maintaining focus on the jack-in-a-box at this age: "You don't happen to look at the right time at the right thing, do you?"

The adult managed the child's involvement with the toy even at the early ages. With infants between five-and-one-half and eight months, the adults often attempted to buffer what they considered to be a potentially frightening event. Some tried to avoid using the toy or letting it pop open, thinking that it might scare the baby. (Six of the nine adults interacting with babies aged five-and-one-half to eight months did so, but none of the adults interacting with younger or older babies did.) For example, one adult interacting with a six-and-one-half-month-old protested when the jack-in-a-box was suggested: "What if he starts to scream? There's a reason I didn't use it." Another kept the bunny from popping out abruptly by holding a hand over the lid, then letting the lid up gradually (six-and-one-half months). Some adults tried to provide the baby with a warning that something was about to happen (in twelve of twenty-six interactions distributed across all ages), or after the bunny popped out they provided the baby with an interpretation of the event as funny or surprising (in twenty-one of twenty-six interactions distributed across all ages). These adults made sure that their face was visible to the child, and they made an exaggerated laugh or excited surprise face, commenting, "Isn't that funny?" or, "Oooh! What was that?" It is interesting to note that the babies never reacted with fright and seldom with a startle or surprise to the popping out of the bunny (possibly due to their familiarity with the toy) except at the oldest ages, when the babies appeared to mimic mock surprise as the adults did at all ages. It appears that the adults' precautions may have been based on their preconceptions rather than on accurate predictions of the particular babies. Several adults expressed surprise that the baby did not react to the bunny's popping up.

At six to seven months, the adult and the baby slipped into joint attention to the event with an ease that allowed the beginning of cooperative action on the toy. By nine months, the interactions appeared to emphasize negotiations over what game was being played according to what script. The participants continued to interpret eye contact, posture, and grasp of objects in interpersonal terms, but now the joint focus of attention seemed to be taken for granted, and the interaction revolved around determining how to use the toy and what role the child and adult were to play in manipulating it.

The shift in emphasis from maintaining joint attention to managing joint involvement with the toy began at about five-and-one-half months and became increasingly consistent. The adult and the baby began to negotiate how and at what level the baby was to participate in the means-end behaviors of winding the handle to get Bugs Bunny to pop out of the jack-in-a-box, then of getting the bunny back into the box. The adult and the baby participated jointly in managing the handle or in getting the bunny back into the box during most of the interactions after five-and-one-half months (zero of the five interactions between four and five months, six of the nine interactions between five-and-one-half and eight months, and eleven of the twelve interactions between nine and seventeen months).

By age six-and-one-half months, the babies seemed to anticipate the popping out of the bunny and to understand some aspects of the script for playing with the jack-in-a-box. They indicated an interest in participating by reaching for the handle or by putting their hand on the adult's hand and "helping" to turn the handle. Adults often attempted to provide further guidance in use of the toy by assisting the baby or by trying to involve the baby in turning the handle (for example, by putting the baby's hand on the handle and saying, "Now, can Valerie's hands do it, too?"). The adult also contributed to the baby's developing script for the event by warning the baby before the pop-up occurred and by providing an interpretation — excited surprise — of the bunny's popping up.

The babies participated in establishing both the rules and the pace of the game. To do so required skill in interpreting the adult's actions and in communicating their own intent and understanding. Adults who are inexperienced with babies can miss or misinterpret the babies' cues. One adult withdrew the jack-in-a-box, saying, "I didn't like it that much either," as the eight-month-old baby repeatedly tried to reach for the bunny, grunting in protest. The adult replaced the jack-in-a-box with another toy as the baby continued to gaze at the jack-in-a-box. Most of the adults in our sample, however, were quite sensitive to the babies' cues, and the interactions showed reciprocal attempts to understand each other's intent. This allowed joint management of the jack-in-a-box. After one adult had made the bunny pop out five times, a seven-month-old gazed first at the handle, then at the adult's hand. The adult stopped turning the handle but kept her hand on it, and the baby reached for the adult's forearm, looking at the handle. The adult removed her hand from the handle, and the baby reached for the handle, trying to grasp it and pull the box closer. The adult asked, "Would you like to turn this time? I'll help you." The adult took the baby's hand, placed it on the handle, and wound the handle with the baby's hand covered by her own. The baby watched as they turned the handle, then looked up toward the adult, who asked, "Are you watching?" and the baby looked back to the box until they made the bunny pop out.

By nine months, the adult occasionally provided explicit instruction on the workings of the jack-in-a-box. In one case, for example, the baby watched with great interest as the adult turned the handle. The adult slowed the turning until the handle was moving very slowly. She explained, "And that makes him come out." The baby looked at the adult, seeming to notice the slowed turning of the handle. He looked at her with wide eyes and a questioning look, seeming to seek information. The adult nodded and confirmed, "Yeah," and the baby quickly looked back to the handle as the adult explained, "That makes him come out." Just before the bunny popped up, the baby shifted his glance from the handle to the top of the box. When the bunny popped up, the adult squealed, "Oooo!" but the baby looked intently at the bunny without any sign of surprise and reached for it, smiling. Even in this instance of apparently deliberate instruction, the instruction was embedded in an ongoing event. This illustrates how the transmission of information is contained within pragmatic aspects of the communication between adult and baby in the process of handling the toy.

The baby plays a large role in directing the activity. For example, the same nine-month-old had earlier caught sight of the jack-in-a-box and pushed it across the floor to the adult. The adult whispered, "What?" and the baby patted the top of the box. The adult responded to this as a request, asking, "Should we make Jack come out?" In the episode following the adult's instruction on use of the handle, the adult struggled to get the baby's hand off the bunny so that the bunny could be pushed back into the box, then offered the handle to the baby to turn for the first time. At this age, the baby was not able to turn the handle to get the bunny out. The baby's response to the offer involved a series of frustrated yet determined moves—whining and fumbling with the box—that expressed his desire to continue playing with the bunny. Eventually, the baby succeeded in using the adult instrumentally to turn the handle to get the bunny to jump out again. The episode began as the adult turned the box toward the baby and suggested, "Shall we turn it?" The baby patted the box, and the adult, pointing to the handle, clarified: "Do you want to turn it?" The baby grasped the corner of the box and pulled it to his side, then appeared distracted. The adult attempted a new game involving a mouse puppet, but the baby fidgeted and whined. The baby tried to pull the jack-in-a-box toward himself, fumbling and whining. The adult watched him, then asked, "Want Bugs to come out again?" When she tried to turn the box around with the baby's hand still on it, the baby whined and pulled away from the box. The adult moved the box, and the baby grabbed the box again, whining louder. The adult began to turn the handle while the baby raised his hands over his head in frustration and fatigue, but he stopped in midair when the music began and stared at the turning handle. Continuing to turn the handle, the adult asked sympathetically, "Is that what you wanted?" The baby stared at the handle and let out a big sigh of relief. As the music played, the adult asked, "Ready?" and strategically slowed down the music. The baby looked at the adult questioningly. When the bunny popped up, the baby blinked and looked at the bunny, and the adult exclaimed, "Up! There he is!" as the baby reached for the bunny. The adult repeated, "There he is!" Then, the baby looked at the adult, who asked, "Is that what you wanted? Did you want Bugs to come out?" The baby, looking at the adult, grabbed the bunny, pulled the box toward him, and turned his attention to it, now calm.

The baby was determined to play with the bunny since the adult forced his hand from it in order to put the bunny back in the box. The adult's misreading of the baby's readiness to turn the handle led to an extended repair of communication, which revealed the extent to which the baby was directing the focus of activity. The baby used the adult instrumentally as a support for an aspect of the activity that he was unable to manage independently. Together, they structured the play in a manner that extended the baby's developing skills.

Considerable meshing of communication in the context of action is apparent in the interaction of an adult with a twelve-month-old. They developed a finely tuned joint script for managing to turn the handle and putting the bunny back into the box. The baby was intent on studying the toy, and the adult focused on increasing the child's skill in its use. The adult coached and encouraged the baby's participation, and they negotiated the level of the baby's participation through nonverbal signals. At the beginning of the interaction, the adult performed all aspects of working the toy, and the baby concentrated solemnly on the actions, frozen in his absorption. By the end of the interaction, the baby showed extensive knowledge of how to work the toy and how to fit his actions together with those of the adult in this particular script.

In the second episode of working the toy, the adult turned the handle. When the bunny popped up, the baby reached for the bunny's head, smiling, and pushed down as if trying to get the bunny back in the box. The baby continued to push the bunny's head down, but instead of going back into the box it bent forward outside the box. The adult came to the baby's assistance, saying, "Let's stick that little rascal back in there!" and sliding the bunny out of the baby's hand. Keeping his hand poised in the air, the baby watched attentively as the adult pushed the bunny into the box, commenting, "Here we go." Then, saying, "Okay—here," the adult pushed the box closer to the baby with the lid still slightly open. The baby put his hand on top of the box, and the adult said in a gentle, encouraging voice, "Close it up." The baby pushed down on the lid with his hand. Then, the adult pushed down on the lid, repeating the words, "Close it up." The adult then pushed down on the baby's hand on the lid as well as continuing to push the lid down with his free hand.

In the third episode, the baby began to participate in cranking the handle, and in the fourth episode the baby seemed to demand some independence in managing the handle: First, the adult reached for the baby's hand on the crank and helped the baby to turn the crank slowly, saying, "That's it." They cranked together for one rotation, and the adult exclaimed with excitement, "That's it!" The baby gently pulled his hand off the crank and watched the adult crank faster and faster. The baby grabbed the box on its sides and shoved it back and forth on the tray, and the adult paused in cranking. The baby looked at the crank and slowly reached for it, confirming the adult's interpretation that he had been demanding a turn. Putting the baby's hand on the crank and turning the crank, the adult said, "Okay now, you do it." The baby again pulled his hand away and watched the adult's hand on the crank, giving the impression that he wanted to do it alone. The adult cranked four notes very slowly. The baby gripped the top of the box with one hand and reached for the crank with the other. The adult turned one more note of music, and the baby grasped the crank. The adult took his hand off the crank, and the baby pulled the crank back and forth. The adult encouraged the baby, saying, "That's it, that's it." Holding the baby's hand on the crank, the adult turned the crank one revolution. The baby seemed to lose interest and looked away, but his hand was still held on the crank by the adult. The adult turned the crank one-and-one-half more revolutions, and the box popped open. The adult released the baby's hand and the crank and the baby looked at the bunny with a smile. The adult exclaimed, "Biiinnnggg!" and bobbed his head like a jack-in-the-box. The baby reached for the bunny and pushed it down, and the adult exclaimed, "You did it!" The baby reached for the lid, lowered it, and closed it, demonstrating knowledge of the script. The adult helped the baby to snap the lid shut, saying, "Let's close it up." In this episode, the baby participated in winding the handle, pushing the bunny back into the box, and closing the box, while the adult supported the baby's participation by winding the handle until the bunny was almost ready to pop and by assisting the baby in holding the lid down on the springy bunny.

About the beginning of the second year, the focus of the interaction seemed to shift again. While interactions at four months emphasized maintaining joint attention and interactions between five-and-a-half and twelve months emphasized managing joint use of the toy, the interactions early in the second year came to stress the interpersonal involvement of the participants in a joint activity. These interactions evidenced an ease of communication that focused on managing the interaction as well as on managing the toy. Before twelve months, the babies seemed to focus on exploring the toy and to use the adult as a tool in managing it. But early in the second year, the babies participated in managing the social relationship rather than simply using the more capable person to make the toy work. The adult collaborator became interesting as a focus of attention, not simply as a tool. This was most evident in the advent of commentary by the baby on the joint activity. The "discussion" of events did not involve words so much as it did facial expression, hand gestures, and jabbering with understandable intonation. Rather than simply participating in the activity, the babies began to interact with the adults about it. For example, an adult and a seventeen-month-old were turning the handle of the jack-in-the-box together, coordinating their efforts with ease and enjoyment. The baby looked up at the adult just before the bunny was to pop out, as if to see whether the adult was also anticipating the upcoming event. When the bunny popped out, the baby vocalized joyfully in jabbered phrases as if commenting on the event, as the adults had done since the babies were four months old.

The plane of interaction clearly began to incorporate more symbolic signals between the adult and the child early in the second year. For example, an adult interacting with a fourteen-and-one-half-month-old provided guidance for the baby's attempts to turn the handle largely through confirmation of the baby's efforts and verbal suggestions for improvement — symbolic support rather than physical actions. An adult interacting with a seventeen-month-old guided the baby's attempts to turn the handle with symbolic actions: The baby sat with his hand motionless on the handle, and the adult rotated her hand in the air near the handle, making turning motions while vocalizing the jack-in-the-box tune. A fifteen-and-one-half-month-old intervened in an adult's choice of what toy to use as the adult was about to put the jack-in-the-box away. The child had seemed not to be interested in it, but as the adult tried to find another toy the baby seemed to decide that she would like to play with it after all and indicated her intent with social grace. She quickly placed one hand on the jack-in-the-box, leaned over to the adult to get her attention, and said, "Unh!" with a slight smile. The adult turned back to the baby, exclaimed, "Yeah!" and began to play with the toy. Somewhat later, the adult happened to catch the baby's finger in the box while trying to close the lid. The baby informed the adult of what had happened, looking at the adult with wide eyes and opening her mouth wide, symbolically signalling pain. The adult understood what had happened, said, "Oh!" and opened the lid, releasing the baby's finger.

Such newly developing skill in using symbolic means to communicate, along with a notable increase in persistence, allowed for extended, focused interchanges in which the baby or the adult collaborated on each other's agenda. In the first example, a seventeen-month-old played a role in a scenario devised by the adult: The adult, pretending to have difficulty pushing the bunny into the box (apparently to arouse the baby's waning interest in the activity), said, "I can't push it down." The baby touched the lid, and the adult suggested, "David push it!" They pushed on the lid together, with the adult grunting, "Uh!" and the baby pushing down on the lid as requested. Here, the adult credited the baby with independence and capability. The same thing happened in another case, where an adult credited a seventeen-month-old with closing the lid, saying, "Ooh, she got it down all by herself" even while the adult was pressing down on the lid.

The baby's skill in symbolic communication and persistence in reaching a goal is apparent in one final example, where the adult assumed that the fourteen-and-one-half-month-old baby knew what he wanted, and the baby gave evidence that this was indeed the case by managing an extended set of directions to the adult regarding which toy they would play with. At the beginning of the session, the adult began looking for a toy in the toy box. When he touched the tower of rings, the baby exclaimed, "Aa!" The adult asked, "Aa?", picking up the tower. The baby continued looking at the toy box, ignoring the tower, so the adult showed the baby the tower and again asked,

"Aa?" The baby pointed at something in the toy box, grunting, "Aa... aa..."
The adult reached toward the toy box again, and the baby exclaimed, "Tue!"
The adult exclaimed, "Aa!" as he picked up the peekaboo cloth and showed it
the baby. But the baby ignored the cloth and pointed again at something in the
toy box, then impatiently waved his arm. The adult exclaimed, "Aa!" and
picked up the box of blocks. Offering it to the baby, the adult asked, "Aa?" But
the baby pointed down to the side of the toy box. The adult discarded the
blocks in the indicated spot. Then they repeated the cycle with another toy.
The baby waved his arm impatiently, and the adult commented, "You show
me!" and lifted the baby to his lap from the high chair. When the adult picked
up the jack-in-the-box, asking, "This?" the baby opened his hand toward the
toy, and they began to play.

Summary

We have argued that cognitive development is fostered by the arrangements that adults make for children's learning environments and by the children's guided participation in an activity. In our observations, the child's
understanding of the game script and skill in manipulating the jack-in-the-box
improved over the course of the episodes of a single session.

The role of the adult is to structure the activity so that the overall goal is
met through appropriate segmentation into manageable subgoals and to help
the child to progress toward the goal by completing subgoals at a level appropriate to the child's skill. This social guidance of learning and development is
often managed tacitly without the participants focusing on instruction, but the
structure of the interaction facilitates learning by the child. The guidance provided by the adult does not always involve direct interaction between adult
and child. Adults are instrumental in choosing the objects with which children
work and play, their companions in learning and exploration, and the circumstances of their participation in activities.

The process of guided participation involves joint responsibility by the
adult and the child for the structuring and pacing of the instruction. Over the
course of learning, the child's participation changes as a function of the child's
becoming capable of handling more components of the task. Together, the
adult and the child calibrate the appropriate level of participation by the child,
where the child is comfortably challenged. In our observations, the focus of
interaction shifted from attempting to maintain joint attention (four months),
to managing joint use of the jack-in-the-box (five-and-one-half to twelve
months), to managing the social relationship in the joint activity through per-
sistent symbolic communication (twelve to seventeen months). At all ages,
however, children play an active role in their own development, putting
themselves in a position to observe what is going on, involving themselves in
the ongoing activity, influencing the activities in which they participate, and
demanding some involvement with the adults who are their guides for sociali-

zation into the culture they are learning. These aspects of social guidance of learning are what we believe may be responsible, on a day-to-day basis, for the rapid progress of children in becoming socialized participants in the intellectual and social aspects of their society.

References

Bernstein, L. E. "Language as a Product of Dialogue." *Discourse Processes,* 1981, *4,* 117–147.

Brown, R. *Words and Things.* New York: Free Press, 1958.

Bruner, J. S. "Intention in the Structure of Action and Interaction." In L. P. Lipsitt (Ed.), *Advances in Infancy Research.* Vol. 1. Norwood, N.J.: Ablex, 1981.

Butterworth, G., and Cochran, G. "Towards a Mechanism of Joint Visual Attention in Human Infancy." *International Journal of Behavior Development,* 1980, *3,* 253–272.

Cazden, C. "Peekaboo as an Instructional Model: Discourse Development at Home and at School." In *Papers and Reports on Child Language Development.* No. 17. Stanford, Calif.: Department of Linguistics, Stanford University, 1979.

Feinman, S. "Social Referencing in Infancy." *Merrill-Palmer Quarterly,* 1982, *28,* 445–470.

Greenfield, P. M. "A Theory of the Teacher in the Learning Activities of Everyday Life." In B. Rogoff and J. Lave (Eds.), *Everyday Cognition: Its Development in Social Context.* Cambridge, Mass.: Harvard University Press, in press.

Lempers, J. D. "Young Children's Production and Comprehension of Nonverbal Deictic Behaviors." *Journal of Genetic Psychology,* 1979, *135,* 93–102.

Ochs, E. "Introduction: What Child Language Can Contribute to Pragmatics." In E. Ochs and B. Schieffelin (Eds.), *Development Pragmatics.* New York: Academic Press, 1979.

Rogoff, B. "Social Guidance of Cognitive Development." In E. Gollin (Ed.), *Colorado Symposium on Human Socialization: Social Context and Human Development.* New York: Academic Press, in press.

Scollon, R. *Conversations with a One-Year-Old.* Honolulu: University Press of Hawaii, 1976.

Sorce, J. F., Emde, R. N., and Klinnert, M. "Maternal Emotional Signaling: Its Effect on the Visual Cliff Behavior of One-Year-Olds." Unpublished manuscript, 1981.

Vygotsky, L. S. *Thought and Language.* Cambridge, Mass.: M.I.T. Press, 1962.

Vygotsky, L. S. *Mind in Society: The Development of Higher Psychological Processes.* Cambridge, Mass.: Harvard University Press, 1978.

Wertsch, J. V. "From Social Interaction to Higher Psychological Processes: A Clarification and Application of Vygotsky's Theory." *Human Development,* 1979, *22,* 1–22.

Wood, D. J. "Teaching the Young Child: Some Relationships Between Social Interaction, Language, and Thought." In D. R. Olson (Ed.), *The Social Foundations of Language and Thought.* New York: Norton, 1980.

Barbara Rogoff is associate professor of developmental psychology at the University of Utah and a Kellogg National Fellow. Catherine Malkin and Kathleen Gilbridge are graduate students in developmental psychology at the University of Utah.

This chapter presents a more general view of the zone of proximal development than ordinarily encountered in the American psychological literature. It refers to Soviet influence on Vygotsky and presents examples from work, play, and educational activities involving elementary-school-age American children.

Current Activity for the Future: The Zo-ped

Peg Griffin
Michael Cole

Translation from one conceptual system to another is always a risky business. When the translation 'crosses cultural boundaries, the risks are even greater. In this chapter, we examine Lev Vygotsky's concept of the zone of proximal development (*zona blizhaishego razvitiya*) for aspects that have been underplayed or overlooked in most English-language discussions. It is our impression that English-speaking scholars interpret the concept more narrowly than Vygotsky intended, robbing it of some of its potential for enabling us to understand the social genesis of human cognitive processes and the process of teaching and learning in particular. The standard source for discussion of the zone of proximal development (Zo-ped) is Vygotsky's monograph *Language and Thought* published posthumously in 1934 and translated into English in 1962. As pointed out by Graham (1971) and Kozulin (in press), the translators omitted material that they considered irrelevant, so that the English-language version contains only 153 pages, while the Russian original had 318 pages. Additional

This work was supported in part by a grant from the Carnegie Corporation DC15 Dept. 06/84–Cole and in part by a grant from the Office of Education DEG008002239–Cole. We wish to thank the faculty, staff, and postdoctoral fellows and graduate and undergraduate members of the Laboratory of Comparative Human Cognition who have contributed enormously to our work.

B. Rogoff, J. V. Wertsch (Eds.). *Children's Learning in the "Zone of Proximal Development."*
New Directions for Child Development, no. 23. San Francisco: Jossey-Bass, March 1984.

45

discussions are contained in Vygotsky (1978) and other sources, but these, too, represent compilations from the original.

Vygotsky defined the Zo-ped as the difference between a child's "actual developmental level as determined by independent problem solving" and the level of "potential development as determined through problem solving under adult guidance or in collaboration with more capable peers" (1978, p. 86). At the time when this definition was offered—the early 1930s—Vygotsky was director of the Institute of Pedology, whose mission was a little like one of the National Institute of Education's centers, since it was charged with translating basic research into pedagogical practice. IQ tests imported from Western Europe were being widely applied in the U.S.S.R., and Vygotsky was attacking the manner of their use, arguing that standardized tests give a picture only of completed development, information of little use in the all-important task of instruction. It was the duty of the school system, he believed, to bring out the full potential of every child. This task could not be accomplished by assuming that completed development fully specifies a trajectory for the future. The standardized assessment strategy leads to a false understanding of the relation between development and instruction, which converts the school system into a vast selection machine. Many nineteenth-century Russian thinkers, including Tolstoy, argued that education should be a transforming experience. Their arguments had a great deal in common with the educational philosophy that came to be championed by John Dewey in the early decades of this century in the United States. From this perspective, "Instruction is good only when it proceeds ahead of development, when it awakens and rouses to life those functions which are in the process of maturing or in the zone of proximal development. It is in this way that instruction plays an extremely important role in development" (Vygotsky, 1956, p. 278).

American Analogies to the Zo-ped

In recent years, a variety of concepts have been introduced into the American developmental literature that are easily interpreted as alternative formulations of the Zo-ped concept.

Next-Step Versions of the Zo-ped. During the 1960s, several American theorists advanced the notion that children's development could be enhanced if their environments provided just the right amount of discrepancy between their prior achievements and present demands (Hunt, 1961). Very similar ideas have been put forth more recently by Turiel (1972) and others. For instance, Siegler (1981; Siegler and Richards, 1981) provides an analysis of the sequential steps involved in understanding classic time-distance-rate problems. Effective training, which focuses on the next step, contrasts with ineffective training, which goes too far beyond the child's current ability.

An important way in which the idea of Zo-ped differs from the next-step formulations is that Zo-peds are expected to embody several levels of the task at once, both next steps and previous steps. Real-life settings, unlike the laboratory tasks that are used for analytic clarity, seem better served by the notion that the child is in an apprenticeship situation where adults create and support several levels of participation. In such situations, development is more appropriately viewed as changes in responsibility for certain steps than as their presence or absence (Kaye, 1982; Laboratory of Comparative Human Cognition, 1981; Lave, 1983). Next-step versions of the Zo-ped also have a built-in limitation for those investigating the possibility of social origins of mental functions. A stepwise progression where the environment serves only as a "trigger" (Fodor, 1983) for the maturing child and a stepwise progression where an adult "scaffolds" next steps are difficult to differentiate on empirical grounds.

Scaffolding. A widely used notion that appears to bear a strong resemblence to the Zo-ped concept is the notion of scaffolding, introduced a decade ago by Bruner and Wood and applied by several researchers who were interested in the way in which the environment helps to arrange for next stages of development. The basic notion is that "adult tutorial interventions should be inversely related to the child's level of task competence — so, for example, the more difficulty the child had in achieving a goal, the more directive the interventions of the mother should be" (Wood, 1980, p. 284).

A good many authors use the notion of scaffolding as if it were synonymous with the idea of a Zo-ped. For many purposes, it may be. Certainly, when the task is to build a tower of blocks, the notion of scaffolding comes easily to mind as a metaphor. But, scaffolding — bolted together tiers of boards upon which human workers stand to construct a building — admits for more easily of variation in amount than in kind. Yet, the changes in adult support ordinarily reported in scaffolding research point to qualitatively distinct kinds of support: Sometimes, the adult directs attention. At other times, the adult holds important information in memory. At still other times, the adult offers simple encouragement. The metaphor becomes more problematic when we focus not on the execution of a specific task but on the changes in the child. A central notion shared by Vygotsky, Dewey, and theorists who use the scaffolding notion is that the discovery of new goals is central to the process of development. To capture the important way in which adult understanding of goals structures the sequence of activities, we would need to add architects and foremen to the building process that scaffolding indexes. Building would have to begin with all the scaffolding in place, and it would have to admit of work starting with the uppermost reaches of the roof as well as the basement.

The scaffold metaphor leaves open questions of the child's creativity. If the adult support bears an inverse relation to the child's competence, then there is a strong sense of teleology — children's development is circumscribed by the adults' achieved wisdom. Any next-step version of the Zo-ped can be of similar concern, including work that we have done.

With these concerns about limitations on Vygotsky's expression of his concept and limitations in current American work related to it, our work has taken two turns: First, we have taken an interest in literature related to the Zo-ped that allows us to escape the largely spatial metaphor, in which the temporal aspect of the construction of the whole remains as a residual, unanalyzed aspect of the living process. Second, we have taken an interest in less well-sequenced tasks and in activities in which adults have more ambiguous roles and abilities.

Some Russian Concepts Related to Zo-ped

As we have become exposed to the broad range of Russian scholarship during the 1920s and 1930s, we have become better able to appreciate the close connection between the development of Vygotsky's sociohistorical approach to psychology and developments in other fields of Soviet science and the arts. Two connections that have been made explicit in the work of Alexander Luria, Vygotsky's student and colleague, were the importance of the theory of motor control being developed by Nicholas Bernstein (1966) and the concept of a functional system developed by Peter Anokhin (1969). (As Luria (1978) explains in his autobiography, Vygotsky and Luria were initiating experiments in neuropsychology as early as 1928.)

Nicholas Bernstein was a physiologist who became famous in the Soviet Union for his studies of the organization of movement and for his insistence on the centrality of feedback. One of Bernstein's most important principles was that the movements of living organisms are organized in time as well as in space: "The fact that they [movements] do not exist completely at any given moment but unfold in time, the fact that they include in their existence the time coordinate in a somewhat different fashion than, for example, anatomical organs and tissues by no means removes them from the ranks of objects studied morphologically. On the contrary, the idea that movement is, in many respects, like an organ (existing, as do anatomical organs, in a coordinate system of x, y, z, t) is extremely fruitful" (Bernstein, 1966, p. 178).

Living organisms are active creatures that find themselves in objective situations of enormous complexity. Since no two situations and no two movements ever repeat themselves precisely, Bernstein maintained that living movement is always created anew at each new moment in time and controlled by feedback. The existence of feedback in turn implies the existence of some "model of the future" that can "feed back" to the present. Bernstein spoke of the concurrent necessity of two forms of models: models of the past and models of the future. Living movement is a process of resolving the information from these two sources. At this point, space comes back into the picture, because the living organism that does the resolving must engage in activity in space in order to resolve the contradictions between what it remembers and what it expects.

Including Bernstein in the discussion, we see that the Zo-ped includes models of a future, models of a past, and activities that resolve contradictions between them. Furthermore, we see a way to make theoretical sense of variations along the temporal coordinate. That is, next steps can be varied for theoretical and practical, educational profit. Creativity is an obvious property of the system from Bernstein's perspective, and convergence is the relatively unexpected outcome which must be explained.

A second concept, implied by Bernstein's work but elaborated by the psychologist-physiologist P. K. Anokhin (1969), is that of the functional system. This concept was used heavily by Alexander Luria, who pointed out that the term *function* is often used to refer to a particular tissue. For example, production of insulin is the function of the pancreas, planning is the function of the frontal cortex, and so forth. Luria repeatedly warned against such simple analogies. Using an example from Anokhin, Luria (1978) pointed out that the "function of respiration" cannot refer to a particular tissue because the whole process of respiration is carried out by a functional system consisting of several elements, including motor, sensory, and automatic nervous systems, the circulatory system, and so on. Functional systems are distinguished not only by the complexity of their structure but also by the flexibility of the roles played by the constituents. So, for example, in cases of injury to the diaphragm, which ordinarily makes possible the intake and expulsion of air, intercostal muscles in the chest can take over and ensure the essential goal of the system—the intake of oxygen and the expulsion of carbon dioxide.

We can see this idea working strongly in Vygotsky when he says, "I have attempted to demonstrate that the course of child development is characterized by a radical alteration in the very structure of behavior; at each stage, the child changes not only her response but carries out that response in new ways, drawing on new instruments of behavior and replacing one psychological function by another" (1978, p. 72–73). From Anokhin and Luria, we can see that the constituents of a Zo-ped, as aspects of a functional system, will have flexible roles. The material, the task, the adults, the children, the models of the future, the models of the past, and the temporal arrangements all function together, as the needs and opportunities arise, to perform the function of development. The reorganization that Vygotsky posits on the internal plane and on the ontogenetic level can be seen operating on the interpsychological plane and microgenetically.

Finally, we also need to introduce the idea of leading activity. A. N. Leont'ev (1981), who worked closely with Luria and Vygotsky in the development of the sociohistorical school, is especially important in this regard. His starting point was Marx's notion that a science of humankind must begin from an analysis of the concrete activities that are the immediate conditions for the development of consciousness. He put the matter as follows: "In studying development of the child psyche, we must therefore start by analyzing the development of the child's activity, as this activity is built up in the concrete conditions of its life. . . . Life or activity as a whole is not built up mechanically, however, from separate types of activity. Some types of activity are the leading ones at a given stage and are of greatest significance for the individual's subsequent development, and others are less important. Some play the main role in development and others a subsidiary one. We can say, accordingly, that each stage of psychic development is characterized by a definite relation of the child to reality that is the leading one at that stage and by a definite, leading type of activity" (1981, p. 395).

Important to Leont'ev's concept is the notion of the parallellogram of development. Figure 1 sketches this construct. The lower two sides of the parallelogram in Figure 1a (solid lines) indicate performance under everyday circumstances; the upper two sides (dotted lines) characterize performance when the subject is acting within the current leading activity. The point of greatest divergence between the two lines is where the subject for whom this activity is a leading activity reorganizes his or her prior functioning. Subjects for whom this is not a leading activity have either incorporated it into their everyday functioning and therefore are already acting in the reorganized way, or they are impervious to the sort of opportunity that this activity Zo-ped offers. Figure 1a shows a parallelogram plotted against age and performance coordinates. Figure 1b shows the sequence of parallelograms and the sequence of transformations of the everyday that Leont'ev and his co-workers have proposed.

**Figure 1a. A Parallelogram of Development:
Dotted Line Indicates Leading Activity.
Mid Age Group in Zo-ped**

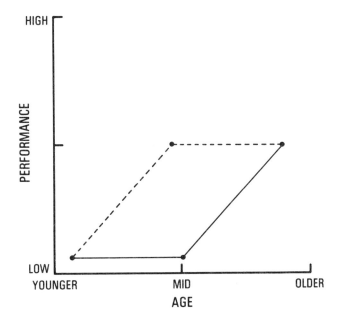

Figure 1b. Successive Leading Activity; Reorganization of Everyday Functioning

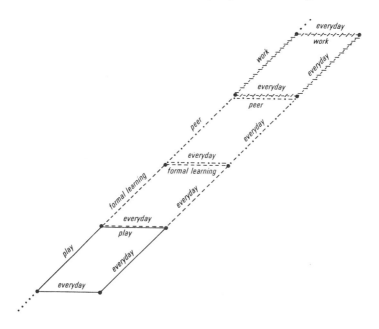

Recent publications (Wertsch, 1981) provide detailed information on the Soviet theory of activity. Our interest highlights three points: First, as an alternative to internal, individual stage approaches to the study of development, leading activities provide for a notion of societally provided progressions, the sort of context-selection mechanisms that we have considered important for understanding development (Laboratory of Comparative Human Cognition, 1981). Second, the "leading" notion provides a framework for uniting several important aspects of development: Variations in the frequency of experiences can be related to changes in kind of psychological activity. Changes in leading activities can be related to the reorganization of constituent actions and operations internally and interpsychologically. The appearance of new leading activities provides for the emergence of new functional systems. As a new leading activity appears, it provides for the reorganization and internalization of prior stages by transforming them into the everyday, in contrast to the new leading activity. Third, just as a fuller notion of the Zo-ped allows one to experiment with the reordering of steps for theoretical and practical gain, so it allows one to experiment with the reordering of the cardinal progressions between the parallelograms of development provided by leading activities. In the sections that follow, we will give several examples of research on teaching, learning, and development using the notion of Zo-ped combined with the idea of functional systems operating over time and the acceptance of leading activity as an important grounding for the study of the process of development.

The Zo-ped in Educational Activity

Within the domain of reading, several decades of research have resulted in a refined notion of the sequence of pedagogical steps that can be arranged to help novices master the mature act of reading with comprehension. Reading is introduced by teaching children to recognize and reproduce letters of the alphabet and to decode words through a phonics-based procedure or through mastery of a sign vocabulary, after which they are introduced to sentences, segments of text, and finally whole texts.

In their research on the teaching of reading in bilingual contexts, Moll and Diaz (1983) found that Spanish-dominant children undergoing instruction in English were introduced to reading in precisely this sequence. Performance among these students was generally below the grade level for English-dominant children within the school district, and both the children and their teacher viewed the process as a struggle. The only remarkable thing about this situation was that, when some of the same students were observed in a Spanish-language environment, they manifested a reading ability several grade levels above the level at which they were working in the English classroom. Instead of spending their hours of reading instruction working on phonics and word decoding, these children were doing rather complicated comprehension exercises, including the writing of book reports on materials at the fourth-grade level. Moll and Diaz were struck by the incongruity of children who were simultaneously too illiterate to read in a language that they could speak (English) and literate in another language, so they decided to test the notion that the children's reading level in Spanish was a reasonable estimate of their independent reading ability. That is, their reading level was the top of a Zo-ped that could not be sustained in an English-language setting because the criterion for next steps in reading presupposed correct phonetic renditions of individual words. In their terminology, the demand to create correct oral renditions of English words pushed the children to the bottom of the Zo-ped for reading as comprehending, which gave a false impression of their ability to interpret the English text and which created a very difficult environment for further instruction.

The intervention designed by Moll and Diaz applied the notion that support with a Zo-ped need not follow a strict task analysis of levels of difficulty. Assuming that the children could read at the fourth-grade level, they used a fourth-grade reader. Children read the material in English, but they were not restricted to English in their discussion of the text, since Moll and Diaz, highly Spanish-English bilinguals, were the teachers. They mixed Spanish and English oral language freely so long as the topic remained the meaning of the English text. Currently, Moll and Diaz are working with teachers and school system officials to reorganize instruction for these students to accelerate their acquisition of reading in both Spanish and English. When the burden of constructing phonetically and grammatically correct oral versions of a response was removed from the children, they exhibited a very clear ability to engage successfully in the task of comprehending the English text.

In Soviet developmental psychology, education (formal learning) becomes the dominant activity, following play and preceding peer activity or work. The principle of functional reorganization with Zo-peds can also be applied to the functional reorganization of activity systems. In the examples that follow, play, work, and peer activities become contexts that reorganize performance in domains usually found in schools.

Play Activity

New microcomputer technology has a potential to contribute to systems of play activity. With it, we can make little fantasy worlds in which children can assume powerful positions as they encounter interesting dilemmas. The television screen, the keyboard, the game paddles, the children, and the adults are recruited into the microworld and transformed, courtesy of a nicely designed program and material social supports in the environment. As in the work by Istomina (1975) and Manuilenko (1975), the most interesting transformation results in the child's becoming able to perform better than he does under other circumstances. Their experiments demonstrated the role of play activity in increasing the child's memory capabilities. Our experiments investigate the role of play activity in children's learning of school tasks, particularly of their learning to estimate along a number line.

In the following paragraphs, we show some of the details of one such activity. At the beginning of the incident reported, Kalani has no visible access to the properties of a number line or to the skill of estimating that a number line can support. His responses are not controlled by arithmetic concepts. The play activity with a peer and an adult brings him to a superior level of performance and to a position where he can independently both rely on properties of the number line and engage in estimation to respond to the task. Like many of the children with whom we work, Kalani often finds it difficult to coordinate with adults in outright educational activities. In a play setting, he can initiate and regulate the adult help that he needs to regulate and stimulate his own mental activity and development.

The Setting. We are in The Fifth Dimension, a world ruled over by the Wizard. (We invented The Fifth Dimension as a device to organize the children's activities with microcomputers without imposing a schoollike control structure. See Laboratory of Comparative Human Cognition, 1982, for a description of its genesis.) Children and little figurines that are their personas are allowed to enter this world, which consists of twenty-one rooms, each a trap or an opportunity, depending on the Wizard's disposition and the child's performance. Kalani is a citizen of The Fifth Dimension. His co-participants, Mr. C and a peer, John, cannot act alone in The Fifth Dimension; they do not even exist there without Kalani's intervention. Kalani and his figurine survive and get transformed by passing from room to room until they reach a room that has a door to the outside. Kalani can reenter with a transformed figurine and try to survive in each and every room. In each room, there is something different to do. Most of these things involve microcomputers, but some require physical games or trips to other places. The activities range from arcadelike games to word processing and mathematical calculations. Each activity has tasks at three levels. If Kalani chooses a high level and accomplishes the task, then he and his figurine have more control over their future: Kalani can choose which of several doors to leave the room by, and he can even get some free passes to bypass some rooms on his way.

The Play Activity Within the Play Activity. Kalani is in a room in The Fifth Dimension. It is another play activity, a microworld, where Kalani is on the ocean in danger of being attacked by a shark. He can use sonar or radar or a harpoon to meet the challenge. Whichever he chooses, the program designers— Jim Levin and his colleagues at the Laboratory of Comparative Human Cognition (LCHC)—have arranged it so that Kalani is faced with estimation tasks on two number lines, where only the end points have number values that appear on the computer's screen initially. One line is vertical, and one is horizontal. One line is called Aim in the game world, and the other line is called Distance. The shark is located at the intersection of these lines, and Kalani must find it by using his knowledge of the number line and by using his estimation skills.

As a Fifth Dimension host, Kalani is obligated to engage his young friend John in the activity. He takes the first turn, estimating where the shark is in terms of the Aim coordinate. John is given the Distance coordinate. John, as a visitor, is unfamiliar with the game and the equipment; Kalani and Mr. C help him out. When the children's estimate is registered, it is quite far off. The children are a bit dejected when they see that they have missed the shark, but they quickly set up to try again. Again and again, they try with little success.

Mr. C (and the researchers viewing the computer and video data later) notice something more. While Kalani takes his turns quickly and easily, neither child appears to have access to a strong representation of the number line or strong estimation skills. Occasionally, with luck or skillful intervention by Mr. C, they get a shark and start out on another hunt, but they show no reliance on well-developed arithmetic concepts and skills. It appears that Kalani has good access to the game world (the goal of the task, the sequence of events, and the equipment). He, as the person in charge, contradicts Mr. C and rejects advice about these matters. John, however, is clearly uncertain about what is going on. The children maintain a high level of interest and use words that suggest that they are "in the game" — they talk of the shark and of firing, not about the computer or school arithmetic.

Mr. C's hints augment the hints provided in the program that appear on the screen. As he talks to the boys, he also interprets the feedback provided for successful and unsuccessful trials in more depth. In both modes, Mr. C uses an estimation procedure that relies on bisection of the number line and landmark estimates. He does not refer to a counting strategy although the "hops" of the lines during the children's turn can be counted. (There are numbers on the screen that mark particular points on each number line — the end points and the points of the child's past incorrect guesses — and these numbers can be used to count up or down from.) Nevertheless, in spite of Mr. C's interventions, Kalani has trouble. He moves the wrong way: Trying to find a smaller number than his last shot, he goes toward a bigger number, but the Zo-ped emerges:

Kalani: (The Aim line endpoints are twenty-three and forty-two in this game, at Kalani's choice.)

Mr. C: Kalani was too high. I'd say Kalani needs to be about...

Kalani: (moving and firing before Mr. C finishes)

Mr. C: Oh, I betcha that's wrong!

Kalani: How do you know? (shouted and sarcastic)

Mr. C: 'Cause I understand the number line.

Kalani: Uhhh. Huh. (It is John's turn, and Mr. C helps. They miss the shark.)

Kalani: I need to make a bigger number, don't I? (Kalani has always talked about a number target, not whether it was bigger or smaller than the last try.)

Mr. C: No, you need to make a smaller number, Kalani. You're shooting way up here on Aim, almost up to forty.

Kalani: Twenty-three?

Mr. C: Why don't you try... Well, here's twenty-three down here.

Kalani: (laughing softly) No, no, not twenty-three!
(Mr. C suggests thirty, and Kalani moves his line in the proper direction. After a lot of help with John's turn, they find they have still missed. During John's turn, Kalani agrees with Mr. C about which way is the right direction, disagreeing only in the estimation of how much smaller it has to be. In a collegial manner, Kalani and Mr. C consult.)

Mr. C: Just a little higher than thirty, Kalani.

Kalani: Thirty-two. (said slowly, with slow movements)

Mr. C: Or thirty-three, maybe. (as a comment, not an imperative)
(Another session of John's turn with help from both Kalani and Mr. C. This time, however, Mr. C starts to count the hops that the lines make as John moves from his previous guess. Then, Kalani

takes his turn without help or commentary, getting appropriately a little higher. And so on, until finally they hit the shark. All three shout in jubilation.)

Kalani: (reading the feedback on the screen) Yeah, but look at the number of misses — Six! (They try another game, where Kalani says) We'd better get hints! (Kalani takes his turns confidently, using the properties of the number line and estimation skills and takes over much of the coaching of John. Mr. C continues counting out loud as the screen position changes. Kalani never does.)

Subsequently, Mr. C leaves to attend to another child. Kalani changes the game a bit, taking advantage of the variation in the program, and continues to succeed. But, along the way and without Mr. C's presence, he starts to count out loud. At first, he counts always from the lines' end points, not from the last guess as Mr. C had done. Then, Ms. G passes by and comments, "Ohh, you're going way back there to the end to count?" Pointing to a midpoint that had marked his prior guess and that was much closer to his counting goal, she asks "What about this?" Kalani, now playing alone, even without John, changes his counting strategy to use the closest numbered point as a starting point on the very next move. He achieves success at the highest-level task, and leaves the room with the most possible control over what room he will enter next in The Fifth Dimension.

The Play Zo-ped. Kalani's improvement has several facets. He learned to insert an estimated judgment of bigger or smaller into his procedure of searching for the proper number. He became 100 percent reliable at recognizing and acting on information about bigger and smaller numbers and number line landmarks. (At first he looked for thirty-eight between seventeen and six.) He moved from being able to perform a task with help, to being able to perform the task alone, to being able to help a peer. He moved from rejecting adult help to initiating requests for it and even to accepting it nonchalantly. At the time that his behavior could be said to be random or at least not controlled by arithmetic concepts, he was also quite fidgety and paid attention to whatever else was going on in the room. He even left the scene from time to time. When he was succeeding, he stayed on task and had to be reminded when it was time to leave. Playing in The Fifth Dimension and playing in the microcomputer shark game provided a Zo-ped for Kalani to go beyond himself. These play activities have also provided a place for us in the children's future, as the children find it plausible and fruitful to coordinate with adults who are interested in engaging them in educational activity.

Work Activity

In the spring of 1982, we developed a plan for a summer program of research involving a group of children with whom we had been working since the preceding fall. The children, ranging from third- to seventh-graders, had one thing in common—they experienced difficulty in school (Laboratory of Comparative Human Cognition, 1982). Our experience suggested that the children had a very sketchy and limited view of what their lives might be like as adults. But a view of one's future as a productive and effective member of society can motivate and constrain the day-to-day actions in which one gets involved as a student in school. If we could provide grown-up work experiences for the children in a special summer program, we believed, they might discover the goal of their future work activity as a framework for organizing their academic behavior. We had significant assistance from colleagues in this endeavor. Beyond our fellow members of LCHC (notably H. Mehan and M. Riel), we had assistance from A. Brown and J. and R. Campione, from Illinois, and V. Koltsova, from Moscow.

We arranged for three different sorts of work activities. One involved making television shows, news shows, and documentaries. The functional reorganization described in the paragraphs that follow occurred as the children prepared for and taped the documentary.

Ben, Rex, and Ms. G. As Davydov and Markova (1983) note with respect to educational activity, there is no guarantee that an individual will enter fully into an activity. Consequently, the structure of the activity cannot be claimed to be the sole determinant of mental development. Effective activity may be a necessary condition to create a Zo-ped, but it is not sufficient. In many different activity structures throughout our work with him, Rex, a fourth-grader, proved this point. He was particularly likely to wreck educational activity structures, sometimes only for himself but sometimes for everyone concerned. Ben, a sixth-grader, was often much easier to coordinate with. He entered fully into many activities that we planned. On the occasion described here, however, the emergence of the activity was fraught with difficulty for all concerned. When it did appear, however, the children went beyond themselves in their performance. A Zo-ped had been created, they organized themselves, and they even took on the responsibility of organizing help from the adult.

The observation started thirty minutes before the boys were to be on camera for the work of making a documentary film about the camp. The three participants were gathered in an office at the university's media center, just down the hall from the impromptu recording studio. It was midmorning on the last day of camp. We provided a tape recorder, a typewriter, materials on which to write a script and cue cards, and materials to assist in planning the presentations—memory prompts about the camp's various activities and possible categories for evaluation of them.

At first, only Ms. G showed any positive engagement with the work activity. Ben had a very heavy cashbox—he had been the manager of one of the other work activities, a lunch restaurant, and the children had not yet negotiated the dispersal of their profits. So, of course, Ben and Rex counted money and discussed the decision. They played with the typewriter. They did anything but prepare for the documentary. Their first engagement with the work was to reject the activity. Ms. G brought up their obligations to do the work, the opportunities that it afforded, the audience projected for it, and the potential content for their contribution. Rex and Ben countered her every move. They provided intricate rationales for not doing the preparation or the taping. The materials that could help them to develop a script or practice their delivery were spurned.

There is a five-minute segment where the children are unable to understand Ms. G and unable to remember anything about an event that had happened two weeks before, a camp-out sleep-over. Ms. G runs through a dozen different types of memory prompt to no avail. She had not been there, but people had been full of stories about the event for days. Listening to the tape of the documentary preparations suggests that it was not that the children would not say what they remembered but that they really did not remember. Finally, Ms. G exclaims, "Well, I guess your part isn't going to be a documentary about our camp; it's going to be an expose! All the children were supposed to go to the cookout and sleep-over, but it seems like you two were left out!"

This went on for ten minutes. The resource available to the adult was the work and its conditions. At a precise time, the children would have to enter the recording studio and do their jobs. There was no out; only the children could do the work, and it had to be done. It was the children's story of what had happened during the camp and what they thought had been good and bad about it. Everybody had to meet the time deadlines because of the scarcity of equipment and time. Finally, with just twenty minutes left, the children turned to the work:

Ben: I'll write the sleep-over, okay? You write the first week.
Rex: Okay.
    (Later)
Ben: I'm making a mess here. I need a big blank sheet of paper.
Ms. G: Okay. (gets him one)
    (Later)
Rex: (Trying to read one of the planning prompts, a typewritten sheet with questions and lines for written answers) What does this mean? (pointing to a line of text)
Ben: (Looking where Rex points) It has to mean *of* the first week, because the sleep-over didn't last a week. (This statement may appear obscure, but it correctly interprets the meaning of the text.)
    (Later)
Rex: Do we have to do the whole page?
Ms. G: No, just as much as you want.
Rex: We'll do two more.
Ben: No, we have to be sure to do The Fifth Dimension.

They devised an outline for their presentation and a means to use notes to replicate it on camera. Each child demanded Ms. G's help with remembering, evaluating, ways of expressing, spelling, and writing notes and reading them. She was taxed to the limit of her abilities as the children took on the work. So were they: They knew what they wanted to do and what it took to do it, and they would not settle for anything but the best from themselves.

When they got to the planning prompts that asked the children to look to the future, to say what they thought about how their summer experience related to school and even real life in the future, Rex had difficulty again. He returned to claiming that the audience was not worth making a documentary for. He wanted to talk about hitting home runs in baseball, which had not been one of the summer experiences at the camp:

Rex: I want to say... (He is cut off.)
Ben: You mean like what we'd do next year?
Ms. G: Yeah, or even later.
Rex: (Cutting in, laughing) You know what we should say... (He is cut off.)
Ben: Like in college?
Ms. G: Umm...
Rex: (Cutting in, talking to himself) ... About pitching no-hitters.
Ben: (Also talking to himself) Responsibility.
Rex: What should I put down, man? (plaintively)

Soon, time was up. The two, who earlier had been full scofflaws about the whole enterprise, rushed down the hall to record, one worrying about a frog in his throat, the other about butterflies in his stomach. Only Ms. G got off task, with a comment about bodies turning into zoos.

In the studio, Ben and Rex continued to organize Ms. G to give them help — about personal appearance, style, and basic reading. They asked for repeated practice on their short presentation. They invented a way to mark the script to indicate who the speaker should be. And, Ben continued to organize Rex, to the degree that anyone could. Their final presentation was quite smooth, both children reading not like they usually did, stumbling and using a special "reading intonation," but instead quite like television announcers. The one problem came at the end, as Rex was talking about the future:

Rex: We study ba... (cutting himself off). Wait a minute. In school, we study baseball to go to college. Uhh.

A zone had been created: the work activity structure, the children entering into it, the adult help, and some changes in each child's literacy performance. What the children could not do currently under the conditions of the school, they could do under these other conditions.

Microgenesis of Leading Activities

The examples that we have given so far concentrate on a single leading activity in conjunction with school tasks. However, we also believe that it is possible to show changes in leading activities that follow development sequences within a single setting. In the course of work investigating the role of social organization in cognitive change (Newman and others, in press), we instituted "child only" or peer activities among fourth-graders. In order to do so, we constructed a sequence of leading activities. At one point, we were trying to get the children to engage in a combinatorial logic problem and concretely to make as many pairs as they could from a set of four chemicals. The sessions started out as play, moved into peer activity, and culminated in educational activity.

A Playful Start. Costumes and props identify play in many societies and in many age groups. We provided the children with costumes: small-sized, white, button-down-the-front lab coats. They were still too big for many of the children, but the children, with clumsily rolled up sleeves and coat hems touching their shoe tops, did look like scientists or, rather, like youngsters playing at being scientists. We provided test tubes, test-tube racks, beakers, squeeze-top droppers, and glass rods for mixing, and we arranged them on a table with a cabinet base, like those seen in many movies about laboratories. We also provided the children with a chart for recording experimental results.

The children responded in play. As they were putting on their coats, they started to characterize the activity. They referred to themselves as doctors or as Frankenstein. They made jokes as if they were in medical settings or in a mad scientist's lab. For some groups, the joking continued, although a little sub rosa, as the teacher told them about the task and showed them the equipment. When the teacher told them about being careful of their clothes and about washing their hands in case the chemicals bothered them, the joking surfaced again, a little nervously. We arranged for the teacher to be busy with something else, so she left the children alone. The joking stopped as the children began to organize to do the task without the teacher as a resource.

The Peer Activity. There were two or three children in each of the dozen groups that we arranged. When two fourth-grade girls and one fourth-grade boy work together, one level of the division of the work is easy to predict: The girls do one part, and the boy does another. Other hallmarks of peer organization of this age group also emerge. Friends bend over backwards to give and take a fair share, to have equitable turns. Those who are not as friendly have tussles about the materials and equipment.

Although the teacher's instructions specified what the task was—to make all the possible pairs with no duplicates—the children did not start out doing that task. They showed no orientation to an epistemic solution—no evidence that anyone could know ahead of time how many and which pairs there should be. Instead, they made pair after pair, enjoying the interesting effects produced by their combining actions. They did not plan what to do next on the basis of some "next" combination's being the logical one to do. More practically, the next pair was chosen on the basis of what a child could find or could talk or wrestle a peer into giving up.

For many groups, however, the task emerged from the peer organization. A question would arise about whether one child could have another turn or not, a question that could be resolved by figuring out whether there was another pair left to be made or whether all the pairs had been done. Or, a question would arise about whether a particular chemical had to be given up by a child so that it could be combined with a chemical that another child had possession of, again occasioning a transformation of the task to see whether that pair had already been made or whether some other pairs were left to be made before possession had to be relinquished. It should be noted that the children were not necessarily being selfish. Sometimes, the fairness issue was raised by a child who would not personally profit. But, under such circumstances the task could emerge. Some children turned to an epistemically well-organized procedure for getting all the pairs that were possible from the set of four chemicals.

The Educational End. For some groups of children, the task did not emerge during the peer activity. However, the teacher returned and helped them to answer her questions about whether they were finished and about how they knew that they had made all the pairs that they should have. Even the children who had not discovered the task in the peer activity engaged in it with their teacher's help.

For the children who had discovered and accomplished the task in the peer activity, it became different in the educational activity: The focus was on how the children knew that they had made all the pairs, not whether there was one concrete pair left. The children reported their results in a more orderly fashion, from which an abstract structure could be more easily discerned. The children did not identify their individual contribution to the effort as a way of reminding themselves of the particular event of mixing a pair. Rather, they relied on a logical procedure to organize the mentioning of the pairs and to account for their certainty that no pairs had been left out of the collective effort.

Sequences of Activities. When ontogenesis is considered, the sequence of these three sorts of activities is play, followed by education, followed by peer activity. When this age group is considered, its members can be seen to be on the brink between education and peer activity as leading activities. It is clear that the peer activity provided a Zo-ped in which some of the children could engage in the formal operational task in a way that is not common for fourth-graders. But, it is also clear that the educational activity provided a Zo-ped for other children and for a different sort of analysis for those who could go beyond themselves in the peer activity.

In the analysis, Newman and others (in press) point out that the peer activity is valuable for child, teacher, and researcher because it is an occasion where children can discover the task. In many activities in classrooms, we can only observe children working within prepared goal structures provided for them by the teacher or experimenter. The task is the question, and the environment is managed so that most of the interactions involve answering it. There is little chance for children to find questions that adults are not actively asking (and that they already know the answers to), and there is little chance for researchers or teachers to monitor or promote the children's development in this regard. It appears that play activity is an available mediating device. The role playing invited the children into an interaction with materials and with each other from which the adult's planned task might emerge. The children stopped playing when the costumes and equipment lost their novelty and when the children lost their teacher. They gave up the peer activity when it had done its work — provided them with the occasion to discover, with certainty, a solution to their task.

The Zo-ped Expanded

LCHC has a long-standing concern about the methodology and theory that is required to conduct a serious examination of cognition outside laboratories and schools and to see the variations in thinking with which humans provide themselves as a hedge against unknown ecological presses. Our interest in human diversity is not a commitment to variety as the spice of life but rather to variety as the source of the future. Supported by an examination of the broader context of Vygotsky's work, we are looking beyond the understanding of the Zo-ped as a reaction to inappropriate standardized assessment measures for a variety of next steps.

We have expanded our ability to see gaps — divergences in which development occurs in a variety of leading activities. The adult role in the functional system differs from activity to activity. It does not always provide support for a stepwise progression, and it does not always assume the executive or higher-order functions. We see the diffculties in getting subjects to discover tasks in different activity settings, even in getting them to engage in the activity at all, but exactly these difficulties are the occasions for us to see the movements, the new creations of a developing organism. Adult wisdom does not provide a teleology for child development, Social organization and leading activities provide a gap within which the child can develop novel creative analyses. As Emerson (1983) puts it, a Zo-ped is a dialogue between the child and his future; it is not a dialogue between the child and an adult's past.

References

Anokhin, P. K. "Cybernetics and the Integrative Activity of the Brain." In M. Cole and I. Maltzman (Eds.), *A Handbook of Contemporary Soviet Psychology.* New York: Basic Books, 1969.

Bernstein, N. *Essays on the Physiology of Movement and Activity.* Moscow: no publisher given, 1966. Cited in V. V. Davydov and A. K. Markova, "A Concept of Educational Activity for Schoolchildren." *Soviet Psychology,* 1983, *21* (2), 50–76.

Davydov, V. V., and Zinchenko, V. P. "The Principle of Development in Psychology." *Soviet Psychology,* 1981, *20,* 22–45.

Emerson, C. "Bakhtin and Vygotsky on Internalization of Language." *Quarterly Newsletter of the Laboratory of Comparative Human Cognition,* 1983, *5* (1), 9–13.

Fodor, J. A. *The Modularity of Mind.* Cambridge, Mass.: M.I.T. Press, 1983.

Graham, L. R. *Science and Philosophy in the Soviet Union.* New York: Ronald Press, 1971.

Hunt, J. M. *Intelligence and Experience.* New York: Knopf, 1961.

Istomina, Z. M. "The Development of Voluntary Memory in Preschool-Age Children." *Soviet Psychology,* 1975, *13* (4), 5–64.

Kaye, K. *The Mental and Social Life of Babies.* Chicago: University of Chicago Press, 1982.

Kozulin, A. *Psychology in Utopia: Toward a Social History of Soviet Psychology.* Cambridge, Mass.: M.I.T. Press, in press.

Laboratory of Comparative Human Cognition. "Culture and Intelligence." In R. Sternberg (Ed.), *Handbook of Human Intelligence.* New York: Cambridge University Press, 1981.

Laboratory of Comparative Human Cognition. "A Model System for the Study of Learning Difficulties." *Quarterly Newsletter of the Laboratory of Comparative Human Cognition,* 1982, *4* (3), 39–65.

Lave, J. "Arithmetic Practice and Cognitive Theory: An Ethnographic Inquiry." Unpublished manuscript, School of Social Sciences, University of California, Irvine, 1983.

Leont'ev, A. N. "The Problem of Activity in Psychology." In J. V. Wertsch (Ed.), *The Concept of Activity in Soviet Psychology.* White Plains, N.Y.: Sharpe, 1981.

Luria, A. R. "The Development of Writing in the Child." In M. Cole (Ed.), *The Selected Writings of A. R. Luria.* New York: Sharpe, 1978.

Manuilenko, Z. V. "The Development of Voluntary Behavior in Preschool-Age Children." *Soviet Psychology,* 1975, *13,* 65–116.

Moll, L. C., and Diaz, S. *Towards an Interactional Pedagogical Psychology: A Bilingual Case Study.* San Diego: Center for Human Information Processing, University of California, San Diego, 1983.

Newman, D., Griffin, P., and Cole, M. "Laboratory and Classroom Tasks: Social Constraints and the Evaluation of Children's Performance." In B. Rogoff and J. Lave (Eds.), *Everyday Cognition: Its Development in Social Context.* Cambridge, Mass.: Harvard University Press, in press.

Siegler, R. S. "Developmental Sequences with and Between Concepts." *Monographs of the Society for Research in Child Development,* 1981, *46* (2), (entire issue).

Siegler, R. S., and Richards, D. D. "The Development of Intelligence." In R. Sternberg (Ed.), *Handbook of Human Intelligence.* New York: Cambridge University Press, 1981.

Turiel, E. "Stage Transition in Moral Development." In R. M. Travers (Ed.), *Second Handbook of Research on Teaching.* Chicago: Rand McNally, 1972.

Vygotsky, L. S. *Selected Psychological Investigations.* Moscow: Akad Ped Nauk RSFSR, 1956.

Vygotsky, L. S. *Mind in Society: The Development of Higher Psychological Processes.* Cambridge, Mass.: Harvard University Press, 1978.

Wertsch, J. V. (Ed.). *The Concept of Activity in Soviet Psychology.* White Plains, N.Y.: Sharpe, 1981.

Wood, D. J. "Teaching the Young Child: Some Relationships Between Social Interaction, Language, and Thought." In D. R. Olson (Ed.), *The Social Foundations of Language and Thought.* New York: Norton, 1980.

Wood, D. J., Bruner, J. S., and Ross, G. "The Role of Tutoring in Problem Solving." *Journal of Child Psychology and Psychiatry,* 1976, *17* (2), 89–100.

Peg Griffin is a senior researcher at the Laboratory of Comparative Human Cognition at the University of California, San Diego.

Michael Cole is director of the Laboratory of Comparative Human Cognition and professor of communication and psychology at the University of California, San Diego.

This chapter integrates Vygotsky's concept of the zone of proximal development into a field-theoretical conceptual framework based on the axioms of the theory of open systems.

Construction of the Zone of Proximal Development in Adult-Child Joint Action: The Socialization of Meals

Jaan Valsiner

Following the methodological ideals of the hard science of classical mechanics, psychology at large, including developmental psychology, has developed its conceptualizations of psychological phenomena on the basis of the axioms of closed, rather than open, systems (Bertalanffy, 1981). Thus, the developing child is usually construed by psychologists as an individual person in himself or herself, the importance of whose relationships with the environment is at best mentioned but very rarely studied. This rarity of attempts to study children's development within environments follows logically from the definition of psychology as a science dealing with psychological phenomena abstracted from their contextual embeddedness (Super and Harkness, 1981).

In contrast, the complex structured phenomena of biological and social realities are more adequately handled on the basis of the theory of open systems. The subject matter of research on child development is the interdepen-

The research reported in this chapter was supported by a grant from the Foundation for Child Development in 1982–83, to which the author extends his gratitude.

B. Rogoff, J. V. Wertsch (Eds.). *Children's Learning in the "Zone of Proximal Development."*
New Directions for Child Development, no. 23. San Francisco: Jossey-Bass, March 1984.

dence relationship between the developing child and the environment. The explication of the implicit forms of that interdependence is the task toward which developmental psychology needs to strive. The open-systems approach challenges the traditional quest for prediction of developmental outcomes and the search for the invariant trajectory of development. First, in the case of open systems, the developmental outcome of a system is in principle impossible to predict on the basis of the initial conditions present in the system. Second, the principle of equifinality applies in open systems: The final state (outcome) of a system can be reached from different initial conditions and via different pathways (Bertalanffy, 1950). Thus, if the development of children is conceptualized from an open-systems perspective, it is both unpredictable and variable in the forms of developmental trajectories. The basis of the unpredictability and variability of developmental trajectories lies in the interdependence of children and environments.

Accordingly, an open-systems approach to child development is by definition context-inclusive, rather than context-free. In this chapter, I outline a possible theoretical framework for the study of child development in a context-bound manner integrating Vygotsky's (1978) concept of the zone of proximal development (ZPD) with an ecological frame of reference for child development. That framework will be illustrated by an analysis of child environment transactions in the second year of life in meal settings.

The Structured Nature of Environment

Each and every setting or object in the human environment is both physical and cultural. This is due to the historical development of the means (and the benefit) of attributing meanings to objects, events, and settings in our surroundings. In parallel to the attribution of meaning, many objects and settings in the human environment are outright products of culture, constructed by human beings for some meaningful purpose.

The developing child acts within the structured context of the human environment. The child's actions change the particular state of that context; that is, they transform the structure of the context. The changed context provides the child with new opportunities for action that may have been unavailable to him previously. At the same time, the structure of the child's environment defines the set of possible actions that are available to the child at the given state of the environment. This idea is closely related to the concept of affordance in contemporary ecological psychology (Gibson, 1979, Shaw and others, 1982). Gibson (1979, p. 127) defines affordance as follows: "The *affordance* of the environment are what it *offers* the animal, what it *provides* or *furnishes*, either for good or ill. . . I mean by it something that refers to both the environment and the animal in a way no existing term does. It implies the complementarity of the animal and the environment." I argue here that affordances in settings and of objects in settings define the limits of what actions of the child are in principle possible. For example, for a three-month-old infant, a staircase does not afford climbing. That affordance comes into existence when the infant develops to the point when it attempts climbing. In this sense, the set of affordances defines the niche for the child's structure of actions within the environment (compare Soraci, 1982).

It is clear that the joint determination of the field of possible actions by the structure of the environment and the available action patterns of the child creates the possibility of high variability in the particular forms of the possible actions of individual children, both within cultures and cross-culturally. This makes it important to study that variability — both in the form of interindividual or intercultural variability and as expressed in change in children's actions over time (intraindividual variability) — not in terms of error but as the subject of the investigation. The legacy of the Laplacean tradition of attributing the causation of observed phenomena to constant causes does great disservice in psychology to the study of development. A more adequate study of human actions requires theoretical concepts that are suitable for describing child-environment interdependence in terms of variability. The contemporary state of our science offers remarkably few such concepts. The concept of affordance is one of these few.

However, the changes in the field of possible actions need not automatically induce changes in the child's actual behavior. In fact, the constraints placed on our actions by affordances are quite wide (sometimes extremely wide; see the discussion of this issue in Cutting, 1982), so the change in the outermost limits of the field of possible actions need not trigger the actualization of these new opportunities.

Effectivities are a subset of affordances that are actualized in the activity of the person in an environment. In the case of the developing child's relationships to the environment, the question of how effectivities emerge in the child's actions on the widely affording environment is of special interest from the perspective of developmental psychology. In order to answer that question, the process of the child's transaction with the environment has to be conceptualized. The developing child's relationships with the environment are channeled by other people — parents, grandparents, older siblings, and so forth. The major function of adult-child interaction from the perspective of child development lies in the regulation of child-environment relationships (Valsiner, 1983).

Within the field of objects and affordances related to them in the environment of the child, the zone of free movement (ZFM) is defined for the child's activities. The ZFM structures the child's access to different areas in the environment, to different objects within these areas, and to different ways of acting on these objects. The boundaries of the ZFM are the sites where the ZFM is constantly either reinstated or redefined. The concept of the ZFM has its roots in the field theory of Lewin (1933, 1939). The ZFM is a changing structure of adult-child environment relationships that canalizes (determines the limits but does not rigidly determine) the development of the child's actions in directions that are expected in the given culture. The ZFM is a socially constructed cognitive structure of child-environment relationships. It is socially constructed, because it is based on the system of meanings of the adult members of the culture and because it is the result of adult-child interaction. It is a cognitive structure, because it organizes child-environment relationships on the basis of beliefs and meanings used by members of the culture in their activities. Finally, contrary to the widespread tendency to project cognitive phenomena into the "mind" of a small child, the cognitive structure here is a structure of relationships between the child's actions and the affordance of the objects. The central thesis of the present theoretical framework is that effectivities in a child's actions emerge as a result of the social construction process mediated by the ZFM.

The ZFM is an inhibitory mechanism. Its function is to limit the child's actions in the particular structured environment. Within the ZFM, it is possible to specify subzones that organize the child-environment relationships further. These zones—zones of promoted actions (ZPA)—are subareas of the ZFM where the child's caregiver attempts to promote certain actions with particular objects. The child may, but need not, comply with this effort by the adult. If the child does not comply, no restriction or limiting action by the adult needs to follow. This contrasts with the adult's behavior when the child crosses the boundaries of the ZFM and the adult acts to reinstate or redefine the boundary.

The Zone of Proximal Development

The ZFM and the ZPA are mechanisms through which the degrees of freedom for the child's actions within environmental settings are selectively regulated. Their particular organization canalizes the child's actions in particular directions. However, the relationships between the ZFM and the ZPA are insufficient to account for the social nature of the temporal dimension of child development. Both the ZFM and the ZPA characterize the status quo of the organization of the child-environment relations at a given time and context, but they contain no information about the potential futures of these relationships. Integration of Vygotsky's (1978) concept of the zone of proximal development (ZPD) into the present theoretical framework would extend it to include the future of the child's development. The ZPD involves the subset of possible actions on objects that the given child at the given state of development cannot yet perform independently but that the child can perform cooperatively with an adult. In the course of experience, actions that previously were possible for the child only in cooperation with an adult (that is, actions within the ZPD) become available for him in individual activities.

The three zones under discussion—ZFM, ZPA, and ZPD—can relate to one another differently in particular cases. The ZPA is usually included in the ZFM. That is, the activity of the child that is promoted by the adult has to be within the range of possibilities that are available to the child. However, under some circumstances, the ZPA can be introduced to bring certain activities from outside the ZFM into it — for example, when an adult introduces an activity, such as cutting food with a knife, that previously had not been accessible to the child individually. Here, it is easy to see that the ZPA can serve to restructure the ZFM.

The ZPD is closely related to the ZPA. Indeed, it can, but it need not, overlap partially or totally with it. Parents can attempt to promote certain action patterns of the child at a time when the child's developmental history has not made him or her ready. In this case, the ZPA and the ZPD do not overlap. Parents can also promote action patterns at a time when the child is just becoming able to perform them in cooperation with an adult (ZPA overlaps with ZPD); later, the child will be capable of performing these actions individually. Or, the parents may decide not to promote and not to allow a certain activity that the child would otherwise be able to accomplish with the help of others. In this case, the ZPD lies outside the ZFM. If the boundary of the ZFM is not reset so as to include the set of actions in the ZPD, then the parental socialization strategy eliminates the possibility that the child will develop skills in these possible but unactualized actions.

Canalization of Children's Actions During Meals

The relationships between the ZFM, the ZPA, and the ZPD will be illustrated with examples from the meal setting. Children's meals provide an especially useful structured situation for developmental psychological research, since all aspects of the situation are set by the psychological reality itself. The meals take place regularly, since the children need to be fed. They are organized by a cultural system of rules, like the meals of adults (Douglas, 1975; Douglas and Gross, 1981). The scripts for meals are generally well elaborated in each culture, and children acquire knowledge of these scripts relatively early (Nelson, 1981). The food objects used during meals afford a great variety of actions (for example, putting food into the mouth, offering it to a dog, throwing it on the floor, playing with it, and so forth). Finally, during meals the actors are pursuing definite goals. The child is trying to get satiated, and the adults are attempting to feed the child and to socialize the child into the "proper" ways of eating for the given culture. Different cultures have vastly different social rules of eating that are purposefully socialized. For example, the use of the left hand while eating is strictly forbidden in the Hindu culture (the left hand is used for "dirty," unclean activities, such as cleaning the body), and the children are canalized into using their right hand while eating. Cultural tools that require different manual skills — such as forks and spoons versus chopsticks — have been devised for eating in different cultures. A detailed description of the development of the feeding behavior of North American children is available in Gesell and Ilg (1937).

The findings reported in this chapter come from a study of twenty-eight children from American middle-class families (range of years of education for both mothers and fathers: fourteen to seventeen or more). The children — seventeen boys and eleven girls — ranged in age between ten and fifteen months at the beginning of the study. The children's behavior during mealtime (usually lunch, but occasionally dinner or breakfast) was videotaped in home conditions in all families at least twice at a one-month interval. The course of the whole meal — from beginning to end — together with some time both before and after the meal was videotaped. An ordinary videotaping session lasted for about one-and-one-half hours.

All but one ($N = 27$) of the children in the present sample were fed in a high chair during the videotaped meals. The high chair is a cultural tool that creates a microsetting for both the child and the adult to organize the meal. First, the design of the high chair limits the freedom of the child's action. The child, who is usually strapped to the high chair seat, cannot climb up or slide down in the seat. The child is also limited in the extent to which he or she can turn around and lean forward to grasp objects beyond the tray set up before him or her. As a matter of convenience for adults, the high chair brings the child to the sitting level of other persons at the table. This affords the child a view of what is going on at the table and it exposes other peoples' activities to him or her. At the same time, the child in the high chair can also easily be moved away from the vicinity of prohibited objects that she or he might be able to grasp.

Although the high chair limits the range of the child's freedom of action, it does not eliminate it. A child in a high chair can perform a number of actions: He or she can manipulate anything on the tray, throw anything overboard, turn to the right or left, or try to look down at the floor. Last but not least, a child confined to a high chair can display active protest that goes beyond the tolerance of the adults and leads to termination of the attempts to keep the child in the chair.

The cooperative activity in the meal situation takes place within the confines of the affordance structure of the high chair. The ZFM is defined by the physical limitations of the child's actions, together with the social regulations of actions of the child in the high chair superimposed by the adult. For example, the adult determines whether the child is allowed to smear food all over the tray. If making a mess is not allowed, the adult would intervene in any action by the child that would result in a mess. From the adult's point of view, the meal constitutes a multiple-criteria problem-solving situation: The adult can simultaneously pursue the goals of feeding the child, maintaining the ZFM with regard to messes, and promoting self-feeding skills, which are in the ZPA.

Transfer of Control over the Spoon from the Adult to the Child Through Joint Action Within the ZPD

Spoons are ingenious tools that have been developed in human cultures to accommodate the needs of food transport and preparation. In ontogeny, the mastery of spoon use is achieved over relatively long periods of joint adult-child action. The adult begins with full control over the spoon and uses it to get food to the child's mouth. The end goal for the adult is for the child to use the spoon efficiently without any dependence on the adult. Gradually, control over the actions involving the spoon is transferred from the adult to the child.

Let us observe the longitudinal course of the development of spoon use in one child who was followed from twelve to eighteen months. Sarah was always fed in the high chair in the kitchen.

In setting 1, Sarah was twelve months and twenty-two days old. The meal started when the mother (M) gave Sarah (S) a plastic spoon to manipulate. M used another spoon to transport food from a jar to S's mouth. Subsequently, M put pieces of banana on a tray, and S used her fingers to feed herself, abandoning the plastic spoon. M put the spoon back into S's hand. S threw it away. M took her spoon, set a piece of banana on the spoon, and gave the spoon + food to S, promoting the reception of it by S's right hand. S took the spoon and moved it towards her mouth, while M continued to keep S's hand + spoon + food on track with her own hand. When the spoon arrived in S's mouth, M released her hold. S took the spoon out of her mouth, and M resumed her hold of the spoon + S's hand. S again moved the spoon to her mouth under the guidance of M's holding. This episode characterizes the ZFM-ZPA-ZPD relationship: The meal starts with the reduction of S's ZFM. Sarah is placed in the high chair, and her mother spoon-feeds her. The episode with the spoon illustrates an action pattern that is both within the ZPA — the mother tries to promote Sarah's use of the spoon — and within the ZPD — Sarah can use the spoon if her mother guides her hand to her mouth.

In setting 2, Sarah was thirteen months and eighteen days old. During this meal, spoon transfer from M to S was not observed. S attempted to get hold of the spoon herself and to get it into the jar from which M was feeding her. M kept the jar on the tray but in her own hand, so that S could not get hold of it. M tried to redirect S's attention to the picture of a flower on the jar's label. S's independent manipulation of the jar is off-limits — that is, outside the ZFM — but touching the exterior of the jar is within the ZFM, and in respect to the label, it is within the ZPA. No joint action within the ZPD was observed during this session.

In setting 3, Sarah was fifteen months and twenty-three days old. M was spoonfeeding S from a container that she held on the tray with her left hand. M put the spoon into S's hand and helped S to get food from the container onto the spoon. S took the food on the spoon to her mouth, but M's hand kept holding S's hand + spoon + food until it reached S's mouth. This episode was followed by one in which M allowed S recurrently to dip the spoon into the jar and bring it to her mouth without M's support. Later, parallel feeding occurred: S continued dipping the spoon and bringing it to her mouth, while M took another spoon and transported food to S's mouth intermittently with S's self-feeding acts. Sarah's "dipping" the spoon to feed herself are within the ZFM, and, since mother sets up the situation for them, they are in the

ZPA. Using the spoon appropriately—both for getting food on in and for transporting it to the mouth—is still in the ZPD. In the case of parallel feeding, the ZFM continues to include S's "dipping" acts.

In setting 4, Sarah is eighteen months and twenty-nine days old. S was given a spoon and a jar containing baby food. These were put onto the tray, and S used the spoon appropriately, scooping food onto it and transporting it to her mouth herself. No parental guidance or cooperation was observed there. However, S could not adjust the wrist position in the upward arm movement to bring the spoon to her mouth in a horizontal position. Thus, the spoon entered S's mouth upside down. Toward the end of the meal, the father spoon-fed S the last bites of the food that she could not get out of the jar. Occasionally, S leaned forward in the high chair trying to get to a food container on the neighboring table. Father immediately removed that container away, so that it was clearly outside S's reach. In this episode, the transfer of control over the spoon from adults to the child has been completed. Thus, the spoon-related actions are no longer in the ZPD, even if Sarah's actions with the spoon are still juvenile, as the upside-down orientation of the spoon in Sarah's mouth shows. The other container that Sarah tried to reach is outside the ZFM, and that fact was reinstated by the father's moving it further away from her.

Variations in the Transfer of Control over the Spoon: Context Dependence of the ZPD

Learning to use culture-provided self-feeding utensils—spoons, forks, knives, chopsticks—displays equifinality: All children end up mastering these skills. The individual paths to that equifinal state, however, are vastly variable, as they are constructed in the course of everyday acting by the child and adults in the meal situation. This variability is the result of redundancy. The task—feeding the child—can be accomplished in a variety of ways —allowing the child to use fingers to feed himself or herself, giving a spoon to the child and guiding the child's hand, controlling the spoon and transporting the food to the child's mouth. During the meal, both the child and the adult can alter their methods. Even when the child is able to use the spoon adequately, he or she can revert to finger-feeding. Even when the child can handle the spoon well with adult help, the adult may prefer to retain control over spoon and feed the child more quickly and with less mess than would otherwise be possible. There need not by any consistency in the way in which a mother organizes two consecutive meals for her child. In one case, she may shovel food into the child's mouth herself because she is in a hurry. In another, she may give the spoon to the child and (if necessary) guide the child's action. This potential absence of consistency, together with the redundancy of child-feeding methods, cannot be treated as lack of organization in the phenomenon. Rather, it specifies the existence of a flexibly organized structural mechanism of human action. Table 1 presents the range of organizational forms of meals that were observed in the sample at least once.

Table 1. Forms of Adult-Child Joint Action Occurring During Meals

Form	Description	Actions Afforded to the Child
1.	A takes F by H and puts into C's mouth	a) refusal (C keeps mouth closed; turns head away, spits F out)
		b) acceptance
2.	A takes F by H and puts into C's mouth hand	a) refusal (C drops F from H; gives F back to A; throws F overboard the tray)
		b) manipulation (C manipulates F)
		c) acceptance (C transports F to mouth H or by Sp/Fo if available)
3.	A takes F by H and puts on Tr	a) abandonment (C does not touch F)
		b) manipulation (C manipulates F by H)
		c) acceptance (C transports F to mouth by H or by Sp/Fo if available)
4.	A takes F by Sp/Fo and puts into C's mouth	same as for Form 1, + C tries to grab the Sp/Fo
5.	A takes F by Sp/Fo and puts the Sp/Fo into C's H	same as in Form 2
6.	A takes F by Sp/Fo and puts onto Tr	a) abandonment (C does not touch F or Sp/Fo)
		b) manipulation (C takes Sp/Fo into H and manipulates)
		c) acceptance (C uses Sp/Fo to take F to mouth or disconnects F and Sp/Fo and uses H to transport F to mouth)
7.	A puts Sp/Fo and F separately on Tr (F can be in Cont)	a) abandonment
		b) manipulation (either F, or Sp/Fo, or both)
		c) acceptance (C transports F to mouth using either Sp/Fo or no utensil by H)
8.	A puts Sp/Fo into C's H and F (in Cont or not) on tray, then guides the C's hand with Sp/Fo to F and Sp/Fo to mouth	a) refusal (C thrusts the H free)
		b) acceptance and cooperation

Note: A = adult, C = child, Sp = spoon, Fo = fork, F = food object, H = hand, Tr = tray, Cont = container

Scrutiny of Table 1 reveals that different organizational forms of the adult-child joint action in the task of feeding can put a different emphasis on the necessity for individual action by the child alone. For example, in forms 1 and 4, the child's degrees of freedom of action are limited to the maximum extent under the circumstances of the present task. The child has a number of strategies of refusal available (turning the head away, keeping the mouth closed, spitting the food out, intercepting and diverting the approaching spoon or fork). On the side of cooperation, the only strategy available to (and expected from) the child is acceptance (by opening the mouth on time and swallowing the food). These forms of joint action tend generally to occur earlier in ontogeny, although it is always possible for an adult-child dyad to revert back to them later. The development of adult-child cooperation in feeding tasks is characterized by the emergence of new, more complex forms of joint feeding actions: for example, form 8 (a case demonstrating the functioning of the ZPD), form 7, and form 6 (control over the utensil and the food is transferred to the child). From the child's point of view, these complex joint action forms provide him or her with the necessity for sequentially organized actions. For example, in case of form 7, the child has, first, to take a spoon or fork and extract food from a container (if one is used); second, to move the spoon or fork to the mouth without losing the food on the way; and, third, to insert the spoon or fork bearing the food into the mouth, retrieve the utensil leaving food in the mouth, and swallow the food. This sequence of actions is a complex integrative motor activity that is mastered in the joint action of adult and child during feeding through action that moves through the ZPD into the individual repertoire of the child's actions.

Whatever forms of joint adult-child action a particular dyad uses in feeding situations at a particular time, the flexible nature of switching from one form to another needs to be emphasized. The adult can switch the form (for example, the mother, seeing that the child will not use the spoon without making a mess, can revert to spoon-feeding), or the child can demand that the form be changed (for example, after being fed for a while, the semisatiated child can refuse to open his mouth to accept a spoonful of food offered by mother, but he transports the food to his mouth himself if the food is put on the tray). Such flexibility in adult-child dyadic problem solving is the basis for any dynamic adaptation to changing conditions of the organism-environment relationships (Thom, 1972). In contrast, an organism whose action patterns were rigidly organized (but whose behavior was predictable for that very reason) would be an adaptational misfit and incapable of development.

Conclusions: The Zone of Proximal Development and the Emergence of Skills in Ontogeny

The concept of the zone of proximal development is basically a metaphorical device to capture the nature of interactive processes whose systemic organization results in the emergence of new skills in the developing child. In the theoretical framework advanced here, the ZPD is the concept through which the development of the field structure, which consists of the ZFM and the ZPA, is introduced. Through application of the concept of ZPD, we can think about the basic reality of child development: Certain activities that at time $t(o)$ cannot be accomplished by the child may become possible at time

$t(o + x)$, having been catalyzed by the cooperation of adults. The field structure of ZFMs and ZPAs is constantly changing, particularly in the directions provided by the ZPDs. ZPDs are collective processes that lead to the development of new skills.

The epistemological status of the ZPD should be made explicit. Vygotsky's emphasis on the zone of proximal development coincides historically with the introduction of topological concepts into psychology by Lewin (1936). The concepts of zone, field, and boundary make it possible to conceptualize the variability of psychological phenomena. These terms allow us to transcend a popular dogma in psychology — that which treats the variability of or in a phenomenon as error that conceals the static, fixed truth from the observer. Zone concepts (in contrast to point concepts, such as averages) make it possible to treat the variability of phenomena as the subject matter of investigation. This variability is necessarily limited by boundary conditions that provide structure for the developmental process. For a developing child, the relationship of the ZFM with the ZPD and the ZPA defines the general direction and particular limits of the canalization of development.

A note of caution of the use of field-theoretical concepts is in order. The zone concepts cannot be treated as causal entities in explaining psychological phenomena in terms of linear causality (if cause X, then outcome Y). In the thinking of psychologists, many concepts often wind up becoming causal entities. The majority of explanatory principles in psychology are static entities to which causality for some phenomena is attributed. Field-theory concepts and the ZPD are endangered by a similar possibility (Waddington, 1966). Such statements as "X happened, because of the field of X" remain empty tautologies until the processes in the field that lead to X are specified. Specification of the processes that lead to an outcome is the explanation of that outcome. In this sense, a field-theoretical framework of children's development needs to specify the process relationships of the zone of proximal development with other zones in the field. From our analysis, it follows that the overlap of the ZPD and the ZPA would be an optimal relationship between these zones (parents promote actions that the child can accomplish cooperatively with them but not alone at that state of development). Both the ZPD and the ZPA are preferably within the ZFM. Under these circumstances, we can observe how interindividual processes (joint action) precede intraindividual processes in ontogeny, canalizing the child toward accomplishment of historically (culturally) given objectives of socialization.

References

Bertalanffy, L. von. "The Theory of Open Systems in Physics and Biology." *Science,* 1950, *111,* 23–29.
Bertalanffy, L. von. *A Systems View of Man.* Boulder, Colo.: Westview Press, 1981.
Cutting, J. E. "Two Ecological Perspectives: Gibson Versus Shaw and Turvey." *American Journal of Psychology,* 1982, *95* (2), 199–222.

76

Douglas, M. "Deciphering a Meal." In M. Douglas (Ed.), *Implicit Meanings*. Boston: Routledge and Paul, 1975.

Douglas, M., and Gross, J. "Food and Culture: Measuring the Intricacy of Rule Systems." *Social Science Information*, 1981, *20* (1), 1–35.

Gesell, A., and Ilg, F. L. *Feeding Behavior of Infants*. Philadelphia: Lippincott, 1937.

Gibson, J. J. *The Ecological Approach to Visual Perception*. Boston: Houghton Mifflin, 1979.

Lewin, K. "Environment Forces." In C. Murchison (Ed.), *A Handbook of Child Psychology*. Worcester, Mass.: Clark University Press, 1933.

Lewin, K. *Principles of Topological Psychology*. New York: McGraw-Hill, 1936.

Lewin, K. "Field Theory and Experiment in Social Psychology: Concepts and Methods." *American Journal of Sociology*, 1939, *44*, 868–896.

Nelson, K. "Social Cognition in a Script Framework." In J. H. Flavell and L. Ross (Eds.), *Social Cognitive Development*. Cambridge: Cambridge University Press, 1981.

Shaw, R., Turvey, M., and Mace, W. "Ecological Psychology: The Consequences of a Commitment to Realism." In W. Weimer and D. Palermo (Eds.), *Cognition and the Symbolic Processes*. Vol. 2. Hillsdale, N.J.: Erlbaum, 1982.

Soraci, S. A. "An Extension of the Concept of Affordance to Behavior." *Psychologia*, 1982, *25* (1), 40–52.

Super, C., and Harkness, S. "Figure, Ground, and Gestalt: The Cultural Context of the Active Individual." In R. Lerner and H. Busch-Roschnagel (Eds.), *Individuals as Producers of Their Development*. New York: Academic Press, 1981.

Thom, R. "Structuralism and Biology." In C. H. Waddington (Ed.), *Towards a Theoretical Biology*. Vol. 4. Chicago: Aldine, 1972.

Valsiner, J. "Parents' Strategies for the Organization of Child-Environment Relationships in Home Settings." Paper presented at the ISSBD meeting, Munich, West Germany, August 1983.

Vygotsky, L. *Mind in Society: The Development of Higher Psychological Processes*. Cambridge, Mass.: Harvard University Press, 1978.

Waddington, C. H. "Fields and Gradients." In M. Locke (Ed.), *Major Problems in Developmental Biology*. New York: Academic Press, 1966.

Jaan Valsiner is an assistant professor of psychology at the University of North Carolina at Chapel Hill.

Assessments of individual students' zones of proximal development within some domain provide diagnostic information about their subsequent performance within that domain beyond that provided by static estimates of starting level or by standard ability or achievement tests.

The Zone of Proximal Development: Implications for Individual Differences and Learning

Joseph C. Campione
Ann L. Brown
Roberta A. Ferrara
Nancy R. Bryant

As the other chapters in this volume make clear, Vygotsky's (1978) notion of the zone of proximal development has stimulated a considerable body of recent research. It is interesting to note that two distinct types of research have begun to emerge. Although the primary issues are different in each, they both flow from the general view of learning and development espoused by Vygotsky.

Vygotsky defined the zone of proximal development as the distance between the level of performance that a child can reach unaided and the level of participation that she or he can accomplish when guided by another, more knowledgeable individual. For a given child and a particular domain, this

Preparation of this chapter and the research described therein were supported by grants HD–05951 and HD–15808 from the National Institute of Child Health and Human Development.

B. Rogoff, J. V. Wertsch (Eds.). *Children's Learning in the "Zone of Proximal Development."*
New Directions for Child Development, no. 23. San Francisco: Jossey-Bass, March 1984.

zone may be quite narrow, indicating that the child is not yet ready to participate at a more advanced level than her or his unaided performance indicates. For another child in the same domain or for the same child in another domain, the zone could be much broader; here the implication is that, with proper input, the child could be expected to perform much more capably than her or his current level indicates. In different terms, these are statements about readiness. This aspect of the zone of proximal development—the difference between current and potential levels—has clear implications for both the diagnosis and the instruction of individual children.

With regard to instruction, Vygotsky believed that in most settings adults and children work together to bring the child from his or her initial level of mastery gradually to the most advanced level of independent activity that the child can achieve. This process begins with the adult doing most of the cognitive work. This phase is followed by one in which the adult and the child share the responsibility. Finally, the child is able to perform independently. The "scaffolding" provided by the adult must maintain the social interaction within the child's zone. That is, the child is challenged somewhat by being asked to perform, with aid, at a more advanced level than the current level, but the child is not required to perform outside her or his zone. The important point is that the child is not formally tested or asked to perform unaided until she or he is ready to do so. The transition is gradual, and the adult is careful to maintain the interaction within the child's zone.

This volume contains some impressive demonstrations of the fine orchestration of this social activity as children are introduced to novel aspects of their environment. In addition, in some of our own research (Palincsar and Brown, in press), we have used this portion of Vygotsky's theory to guide the structuring of sets of interactive lessons designed to teach academically poor students to use a variety of argument skills to facilitate their comprehension and recall of science and social science expository tests. (See Brown and Campione, in press, for a discussion of that work in the context of Vygotskian theory.)

There is, however, another way in which Vygotsky used the zone of proximal development. He also conceived of it as a test of the child's readiness or intellectual maturity in a specified domain. In this guise, he used it as an individual difference metric designed to provide supplementary information about individual students. His aim was to distinguish between the child's actual development level, indexed by unaided performance on standard assessments (ability or achievement tests), and the child's level of potential development (performance achievable with aid). Vygotsky viewed the achievement test score as providing a quantitative estimate of current status but only indirect evidence concerning the processes whereby that status was achieved. That is, test scores do not provide any information about "those functions that have not yet matured but are in the process of maturation, functions that will mature tomorrow but are in the embryonic stage. These functions could be termed the 'buds' or 'flowers,' rather than the fruits of development. The actual developmental level characterizes mental development retrospectively, while the zone of proximal development characterizes mental development prospectively" (1978, pp. 86–87). Hence, Vygotsky wished to supplement static test information regarding individual children with information about the processes that they might bring to bear in coming to deal with the domain. This dynamic assessment approach is similar to those described subsequently by Budoff (1974) and Feuerstein (1979). It is interesting to note that Vygotsky developed this portion of his theory when he was serving as director of the Institute of Defectology in Moscow, and where he was faced with the practical task of educational assessment in a wildly unstable postrevolutionary population. Similarly, Feuerstein was motivated in good part to develop his Learning Potential Assessment Device when confronting a similar problem in displaced person camps in Israel. Faced with evaluating children who had spent years without formal education, standard ability and achievement tests seemed quite inappropriate.

It was this interpretation of the zone of proximal development as an individual difference metric that guided the research described in this chapter. We wished to test Vygotsky's assumption that assessments of how students respond to socially structured instruction within some domain of interest would provide important diagnostic information about them. We were interested in both the initial acquisition of information and in its later flexible use. More specifically, we aimed to engage students in an interactive learning situation and assess how much input they would need before they mastered certain sets of problems. This would provide a measure of learning ability within that domain. Following that, we would continue the interactive format and assess how much additional help the students would need before they would use the principles that they had learned in modified formats. This would provide a measure of transfer propensity. Again, the notion is that, even if all children perform at the same (poor) level initially, the ease with which they acquire relevant information and put it to use will allow us to distinguish children who are likely to experience later problems in that area from children who are not.

Vygotsky's point is that, while how much a student knows about some area (as assessed on the static test) is a powerful predictor of performance in that area, children also differ in how efficiently they learn. Estimates of this efficiency will enhance our ability to predict students' later performance. Questions about the existence and extent of ability-related differences in learning and transfer processes have, of course, a long history. Early views of intelligence (Binet, 1903; Dearborn, 1921; Spearman, 1923; Thorndike, 1926) stressed the centrality of learning. Some authors went so far as to identify learning with intelligence. However, many of the attempts to verify such relations empirically produced negative results and evidence for the presumed relation between learning and intelligence was not easy to come by. We have speculated elsewhere (Campione and others, 1982) on some of the reasons for the negative results. They include the conception of learning as an automatic, passive process; the nature of the tasks used to assess learning; and the domains in which the tasks were situated — typically, completely arbitrary ones.

There is, however, for our purposes here a more relevant problem in interpreting early data on learning and intelligence. In the early studies, learners worked independently on the task with no feedback other than knowledge of results. A main point both of Vygotsky's approach and of this chapter is the importance of interactive learning situations that provide structured guidance for the learner. It has been argued that these kinds of settings should be most sensitive to individual differences (Campione and Brown, in press; Cronbach, 1967). There are some data available that are consistent with these ideas. In contrast to the original negative findings, recent research conducted in an instructional context seems to suggest a relation between ability measures and learning and transfer performance. (Campione and others, 1982, review this literature.) In many cases, academically delayed children require surprisingly detailed input before they come to use a particular learning or memory strategy. Further, having come to use it, they are extremely unlikely to transfer it to novel situations. They appear to be "slow" to learn and "reluctant" to transfer.

In the research discussed here, we wished to follow up on the earlier work and to situate it within the context of Vygotsky's developmental theory. The research was conducted in two stages. The first, which involved comparisons among groups of children, was concerned with the relation between learning and transfer processes and global measures of ability. The question was whether Vygotsky's procedures would allow us to distinguish experimentally groups of children experiencing differing degrees of academic success. In the second, we concentrated more directly on individual differences. Here, the question was whether dynamic assessments of the child's zone of proximal development could be used to refine predictions about individual students' progress toward mastery within some specified domain.

Experimental Evaluation of the Zone of Proximal Development

In this research, we used a particular interpretation of the zone of proximal development as a basis for assessing individual differences in learning ability and transfer propensity. A number of factors are common to all the experiments. They all involved observations of performance in inductive reasoning domains in which the students had performed quite poorly on initial unaided tests. In each case, the students were taught to solve various problems requiring the detection and application of a specified set of principles or rules. All students learned those problem types to the same criterion of mastery — independent, unassisted problem solution. Then, the students were given a series of transfer problems to solve. The exact nature of these problems varied between and within the studies, but they can be generally described as consisting of maintenance items — novel exemplars of the problem types learned originally; near transfer items — problems involving the same rules or principles learned originally but in novel combinations; and far transfer items — problems requiring the use of a new but related rule or principle in addition to the familiar ones. An example involving a series of completion problems is provided in Table 1. The child's task in the problem presented in Table 1 is to fill the blanks with the letters that continue the pattern determined by a certain periodicity and by certain alphabetic relations. In the *next* relation, the letters appear in alphabetical sequence; in the *identity* relation, the letters repeat; and in the *backward-next* relation, the letters appear in reverse alphabetical sequence.

The measure of individual differences in learning and transfer efficiency were obtained from the children's response to guided and systematic instruc-

Table 1. Examples of Learning, Maintenance, and Transfer Items

Problem Type	Pattern[a]	Sample Problem	Correct Answer
Original Learning	*NN*	NGOHPIQJ＿＿＿＿	(RKSL)
	NINI	PZUFQZVF＿＿＿＿	(RZWF)

Maintenance (Learned pattern types; new instantiations)

Near Transfer (Learned relations and periodicities, but in new combinations)

| | *NI* | DVEVFVGV＿＿＿＿ | (HVIV) |
| | *NNNN* | VHDPWIEQ＿＿＿＿ | (XJFR) |

Far Transfer (New relation, backward-next, or new periodicity, three letters)

	BN	UCTDSERF＿＿＿＿	(QGPH)
	NBNI	JPBXKOCX＿＿＿＿	(LNDX)
	NIN	PADQAERA＿＿＿＿	(FSAG)

Very Far Transfer (Backward-next as well as next relations and "period" of two letters, but relations must be sought between strings of letters rather than within a string)

Instructions:

Pretend that you are a spy. You want to send the message on top in a secret code that only your friends will understand. Someone has begun coding the message for you on the second line. Try to figure out the secret code and finish coding the message by filling in the blanks with the letters that follow the code.

SIX SHIPS GONE

THY RIHQR ＿＿＿＿   (HNOD)

[a]The letters themselves in the pattern notations refer to the alphabetic relations (i.e., N = next, I = identity, B = backward-next). The number of letters in each pattern notation equals the period.
Source: Adapted from Campione, Brown, and Ferrara (1982)

tion. Following Vygotsky, the instruction in each study was of the same general form. Subjects were set to work on a given problem. If they were unable to solve the problem, they were given a series of hints to help them. The initial hints were very general, but the succeeding hints became progressively more specific and more concrete, with the last "hint" actually providing a detailed blueprint for generating the correct answer. This titration procedure allowed us to estimate the minimum amount of help that a given child needed in order to solve each problem. The metric of learning efficiency was the number of hints required for the attainment of the learning criterion. Note that this metric differs from the one that Vygotsky suggested in that it is not how much improvement one can bring about via a specified amount of intervention but rather how much aid is needed to bring about a specified amount of learning. We used this metric because it proved more amenable to practical considerations, given the tasks involved. Furthermore, as we argue later, the diagnostic picture obtained by means of this metric may be more informative regarding future instruction.

Exactly the same hinting procedure was used on the transfer problems, generating the analogous metric. Note that the index of transfer propensity is thus dynamic rather than static (Brown and others, 1983). That is, we are not measuring how many and what types of transfer items the subjects can solve on an unaided test (a static measure); we are concerned with how facile the subjects are in coming to deal with related portions of the overall problem space (a dynamic measure) — specifically, with how many hints they require in order to solve the different types of transfer problems.

Studies of Group Differences

Series Completion Study. The initial experiments involved comparison of groups of children who differed in measured intelligence. The first involved third- and fifth-graders of average (mean IQ = 101) and above-average (mean IQ = 122) ability (Ferrara and others, 1983). The children learned to solve two types of letter series completion items in the first session, and in subsequent transfer sessions they were asked to solve variations of the original patterns. (See Table 1.) There was a reliable difference due to IQ when the learning data were considered: High-ability children needed fewer hints to learn the initial problem sets than children in the average-ability group did. The transfer data, however, are of more interest here. The major finding is that group differences increased as transfer distance increased. Virtually no aid was required on the maintenance items, and very little aid was required on the near transfer set. In neither case were there any group differences. However, on the far and very far transfer items, group differences were highly reliable. The results of a series of correlational analyses revealed the same pattern. Correlations between IQ scores and number of hints were nonsignificant for maintenance and near transfer, but they were reliable when far and very far transfer performance was considered.

In summary, there was evidence of an ability-learning link, all groups showed clear evidence of maintenance, reliable group differences emerged in transfer, and the magnitude of these differences increased as a function of transfer distance.

Progressive Matrices Study. In the second group comparative study, Campione and others (in press) compared the performance of mildly retarded (mean IQ = 72) and nonretarded (mean IQ = 118) children. One motivation for this study was to extend the analyses of the first study to a group of lower-functioning children; hence, the inclusion of the retarded sample. Second, we wished to compare two groups whose members differed in their general academic ability but who were approximately matched in terms of their initial competence in dealing with the kinds of problems to be studied. The question here was whether ability-related differences in learning, in transfer performance, or in both would be obtained when the students started at an equivalent level.

The two groups were matched for a mental age of approximately 10.5 years. More importantly, they were matched on a task pretest, which assessed starting competence on the rules to be taught and used during the learning and transfer sessions. In this study, the subjects learned to solve modified Ravens Progressive Matrices problems involving three rules: rotation, imposition, and subtraction. An example is shown in Figure 1a. The children see a three by three array of figures, with the lower left cell empty. Their task is to determine the pattern that best completes the matrix. During the learning portion of the study, the problems were presented in a blocked format. Each student learned the rotation problems to a preset criterion, then the imposition problems, and finally the subtraction problems (an easy-to-hard sequence). In the next session (maintenance), novel exemplars of the same problem types (rotation, and so forth) were presented but in a random order. Finally, during the transfer session, these item types were presented again but this time interspersed with a set of transfer problems. The transfer problems required the simultaneous use of two of the original rules, such as rotation and subtraction. An example is shown in Figure 1b.

In all three sessions, the problems were presented via computer. The missing figure in each matrix was constructed by the child, who issued certain simple commands using a touch-sensitive screen. Graduated and animated hints were provided by the computer as needed. An adult read the hints to the child and provided additional guidance and encouragement.

No differences were obtained during the learning phase, possibly due to the matching procedures employed. That is, the retarded and the nonretarded groups had been equated in terms both of mental age and of their entering performance level on the kinds of problems employed in the instructional sessions. The next questions concerned maintenance and transfer. Here, group differences were consistently obtained. Consider first the initial maintenance phase. As in the first study, the nonretarded group showed clear

84

Figure 1. Examples of Matrices Problems.

(Panel (a) shows an example of one of the rotation problems used during the instructional sessions. Panel (b) shows an example of a transfer problem involving both rotation and imposition.)

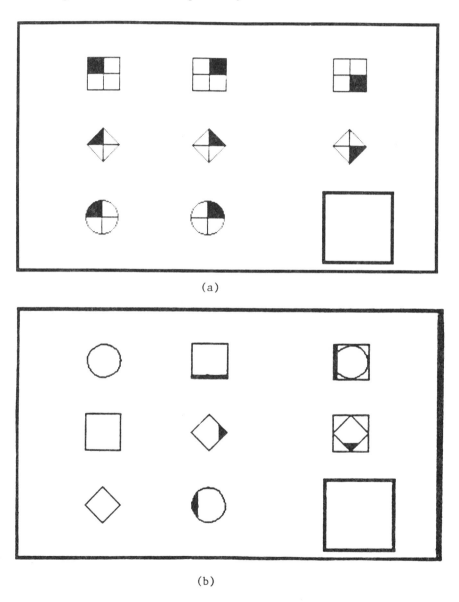

(a)

(b)

Source: Campione and others, 1983.

evidence of maintenance — almost no hints were required. In contrast, the performance of the retarded students was significantly impaired. Although they had eventually learned to solve such items independently (with zero hints) in the original blocked learning session, they again required some assistance when the same problem types were randomly ordered in the maintenance session. The group difference in this session was significant.

The maintenance session differed from the original learning situation in the complexity of the context in which the problems were presented — blocked during learning and randomized during maintenance. This complexity was increased further in the transfer phase, when maintenance problems were interspersed with novel transfer problems. Here, group differences were again apparent, and their magnitude was reliably larger than it had been during the preceding maintenance session. Our interpretation of the maintenance data is that increasing the complexity of the context in which the target problems are embedded increases the importance of problem detection processes as determinants of performance relative to the processes involved in an already identified approach. That is, one factor underlying the retarded child's failure to use information flexibly is the child's difficulty in identifying novel exemplars of known problem types that are not clearly marked by context.

The groups also differed on the transfer items. Although the retarded subjects had learned to use a set of rules to some specified criterion, they nonetheless required significantly more help than nonretarded subjects did in order to solve problems requiring the use of those rules in combination. Again, the conclusion is that, although the two groups learned to apply the rules to the same criterion originally and although they required approximately the same amount of help to reach that criterion, they nonetheless differed significantly on subsequent occasions when they were required to use those rules in a flexible fashion.

If we consider the maintenance and transfer phases of the two studies, a fairly consistent pattern emerges. As the degree of change from the initial learning situation to the transfer probes increases, ability-related differences also generally increase. Also, the lower the ability level of the student, the smaller the change required to generate some disruption of performance. In the study by Campione and others (1983), for example, performance on maintenance items was sufficient to discriminate retarded children from nonretarded children. When children in the normal range of intelligence were involved, ability-related differences were not found until far transfer probes were instituted.

Studies of Individual Differences

In the first pair of studies, we were concerned with differences in learning and transfer efficiency characteristic of groups of children who differed in academic success. Those studies produced data consistent with Vygotsky's overall views, and thus they were quite encouraging. However, Vygotsky was also concerned with a much more difficult problem, the analysis of individual children — specifically with whether estimates of instructionally produced improvements in performance would provide important diagnostic information about individual learners. In the next study to be described here (Bryant and others, 1983), we addressed this issue.

To place this study in context, consider the typical diagnostic setting that children encounter. They are given a test of some sort to assess their competence within some domain, and then several important educational decisions are based on the outcome of that test. Vygotsky was concerned (see also Budoff, 1974; and Feuerstein, 1979) that such tests might underestimate the potential of some individuals; hence, he suggested that each student's response to instruction should also be investigated. The important question is then which measure best predicts a student's later developmental path — the typical achievement pretest or the learning and transfer evaluation.

Bryant and others (1983) studied the ability of five-year-olds to come to deal with a simplified set of matrix problems, samples of which are shown in Figure 2. All subjects were administered a pretest, followed by learning and transfer sessions with the same type of hinting procedures described earlier and a final posttest. All children were brought to the same criterion on certain problem types, as in the previous studies. Then, they were required to solve a variety of transfer problems. Measures of the amount of assistance required to master the original learning and transfer problems were recorded. The interesting findings concerned the change scores between pre- and post-tests, specifically the residual gain score. This score was interpreted as the overall improvement shown by each student as a result of the instructional sessions.

First, consider the results of some simple correlational analyses. We were interested in the extent to which the various measures obtained could be used to predict the residual gain score. The best predictor of gain status proved to be be performance on far transfer items, followed by near transfer indices and learning efficiency. Consistent with Vygotsky's general views, these were all better predictors than the various static pretest assessments. In a somewhat more rigorous evaluation of the hypotheses, the data were also subjected to a number of hierarchical multiple regression analyses, the results of which are shown in Table 2. Although estimated IQ (based on the Information, Coding, Vocabulary, and Picture Completion subtests of the WPPSI) and static Ravens Colored Progressive Matrices test scores accounted for 37 percent of the variance in residual gain, the training (that is, learning) measure produced a significant increment accounting for an additional 22.4 percent of the variance. Moreover, the transfer measure accounted for a further 18.7 percent of the variance in residual gain — also a significant increment. The sets of analyses are thus quite consistent. Assessment of the student's zone of proximal development as indexed by learning and transfer efficiency provides important diagnostic and predictive information about individual students, which is nicely consistent with Vygotsky's theorizing.

Figure 2. Examples of Simplified Matrices Problems and Solution Alternatives Presented to Very Young Children

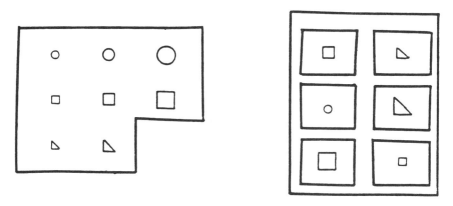

Simple Two Way

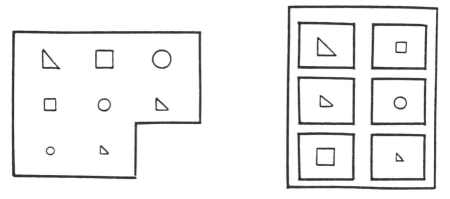

Two Way Underrepresentation in One Direction

Source: Bryant and others, 1983.

Similar results were obtained with young subjects using a simplified series completion task (Bryant and others, 1983). Again, the IQ and Ravens scores alone accounted for a significant portion of the variance (33 percent) in residual gain. Addition of the learning scores did not result in a significant increment due to the substantial simple correlations of learning with IQ and the Ravens scores ($r = -.54$ and $r = -.37$, respectively). The entry of transfer into the equation did, however, result in a significant increment accounting for an additional 20 percent of the variance in residual gain.

Table 2. Multiple Regression Summary Table

Dependent Variable	Step	Independent Variables	Correlation (r)	F to enter	Multiple R	Increment in R²	Overall F	Significance
Training	1	Information	−.439[a]	5.49[a]	.439	.193	5.49	.028
	2	Coding Task	−.043	5.10[a]	.587	.152	5.79	.010
	3	Vocabulary	.024	1.56	.625	.045	4.48	.014
	4	Pict. Comp.	−.072	.56	.638	.017	3.43	.027
Transfer	1	Information	−.389[a]	4.10	.389	.151	4.10	.055
	2	Pict. Comp.	.110	1.34	.447	.049	2.75	.086
	3	Coding Task	−.330	.60	.471	.023	2.00	.145
	4	Vocabulary	−.165	.17	.478	.006	1.48	.246
Residual Gain	1	Estimated IQ	.485[a]	7.08[a]	.485	.235	7.08	.014
	2	Ravens	.472[a]	4.70[a]	.608	.135	6.46	.006
	3	Training	−.605[a]	11.61[a]	.776	.224	10.26	<.001
	4	Transfer	−.598[a]	14.94[a]	.876	.173	16.53	<.001
	5	Far Transfer	−.698[a]	1.22	.884	.014	13.61	<.001

[a]Significant, p < .05
Source: Bryant, Brown, and Campione, 1983.

Thus, the dynamic measures tended to be superior to the static measures in their ability to predict how much young children would profit from instruction. The conclusion is that individual differences in learning and transfer performance are important predictors of performance improvement within a domain. Consistent with Vygotsky's views, even though all subjects learned the original rules to the same criterion and eventually solved the transfer problems, the facility with which they accomplished these steps were closely related to how much they benefited from the instructional intervention; that is, how large a gain they made from pretest to posttest.

Discussion

Static test procedures typical of most assessment approaches dramatically underestimate the level of functioning that a child can achieve. In each of the studies just described, following suitable intervention all the subjects came to solve quite complex problems, including items that appear on the Superior Adult scale of the Stanford-Binet intelligence test. Thus, there is a large difference between what Vygotsky called the actual and the potential levels of development. Children who perform quite poorly when left to their own devices come to do much better following suitable intervention. This information is of obvious relevance to psychometricians who are concerned with evaluating students' aptitudes and abilities. However, it is also of considerable interest to those who study cognitive development. In most of the research in that area, children are assessed in situations where they are asked to perform unaided, and conclusions are then drawn about their cognitive competence. The data reported here suggests that the conclusions might change considerably if some form of aid were provided to the subjects.

The extent to which information about a particular student's zone of proximal development provides useful information beyond that obtained from static tests is also clear. The procedures that we employed were sensitive to group differences in overall academic success and to individual differences in progress within more constrained domains. These results have a number of implications. On a somewhat general level, the data provide information about some of the components of academic success, or intelligence. The studies, situated in the context of social interactional instructional settings, have succeeded in demonstrating a relation between ability scores and indices of learning and transfer efficiency, thereby contributing to the long-standing controversy regarding the centrality of learning processes to theories of intelligence.

There are also more specific implications for the diagnosis of individual children. While ability measures and indices of learning or transfer efficiency are related, the relation is imperfect. Estimates of the facility with which individual students respond to instruction and, even more strongly, the degree to which they show initial evidence of transfer of learned skills do predict the amount of longer-term improvement that they are likely to show, as Table 2 shows. That is, while ability scores do predict overall improvement, the learning and transfer scores add considerably to the overall predictability; in fact, considered separately, they do a better job than the static pretest assessments. Again consistent with Vygotsky's views, the process measures do speak to the issue of readiness. They provide information beyond that available from pretest measures about students who may experience later problems in the domain under investigation.

One immediate benefit is that the use of these procedures may immediately uncover potential masked by poor starting levels. This is important because it would diminish the likelihood that students who could profit from instruction would be denied that opportunity on the basis of initial assessment suggesting that they were not yet ready to undertake work in a particular area. Even for students who do not perform exceptionally well on the process measures, the results of the interactive sessions may provide more specific information about their strengths and weaknesses. For example, in some of our initial data (Brown and Ferrara, in press; Ferrara and others, 1981), students showed a variety of profiles. Some learned quite quickly, but they were not able to transfer what they had learned readily to new problems. Others were slower to learn, but once having done so they transferred quite flexibly. If these patterns prove to be consistent across a number of domains, it would appear that different forms of intervention could be tailored to the different groups of students.

In summary, these data provide an initial validation of Vygotsky's ideas in the area of diagnosis. Coupled with the data provided elsewhere in this volume, the results indicate that the notion of the zone of proximal development can contribute to our understanding of a number of issues of central concern to those interested in both basic psychological processes and the application of research findings to issues of practical concern.

References

Binet, A. *The Experimental Study of Intelligence.* Paris: Schleicher Frères, 1903.

Brown, A. L., Bransford, J. D., Ferrara, R. A., and Campione, J. C. "Learning, Remembering, and Understanding." In J. H. Flavell and E. M. Markman (Eds.), *Carmichael's Manual of Child Psychology.* Vol. 3. New York: Wiley, 1983.

Brown, A. L., and Campione, J. C. "Three Faces of Transfer: Implications for Early Competence, Individual Differences, and Instruction." In M. Lamb, A. Brown, and B. Rogoff (Eds.), *Advances in Developmental Psychology.* Vol. 3. Hillsdale, N.J.: Erlbaum, in press.

Brown, A. L., and Ferrara, R. A. "Diagnosing Zones of Proximal Development." In J. V. Wertsch (Ed.), *Culture, Communication, and Cognition: Vygotskian Perspectives.* New York: Cambridge University Press, in press.

Bryant, N. R., Brown, A. L., and Campione, J. C. "Preschool Children's Learning and Transfer of Matrices Problems: Potential for Improvement." Unpublished manuscript, University of Illinois, 1983.

Budoff, M. *Learning Potential and Educability Among the Educable Mentally Retarded.* Cambridge, Mass.: Research Institute of Educational Problems, Cambridge Mental Health Association, 1974.

Campione, J. C., and Brown, A. L. "Learning Ability and Transfer Propensity as Sources of Individual Differences in Intelligence." In P. H. Brooks, C. McCauley, and R. D. Sperber (Eds.), *Learning and Cognition in the Mentally Retarded.* Baltimore: University Park Press, in press.

Campione, J. C., Brown, A. L., and Ferrara, R. A. "Mental Retardation and Intelligence." In R. J. Sternberg (Ed.), *Handbook of Human Intelligence.* New York: Cambridge University Press, 1982.

Campione, J. C., Brown, A. L., Ferrara, R. A., Jones, R. S., and Steinberg, E. "Differences Between Retarded and Nonretarded Children in Transfer Following Equivalent Learning Performance: Breakdowns in Flexible Use of Information." Unpublished manuscript, University of Illinois, 1983.

Cronbach, L. J. "How Can Instruction Be Adapted to Individual Differences?" In R. M. Gagne (Ed.), *Learning and Individual Differences.* Columbus, Ohio: Merrill, 1967.

Dearborn, W. F. "Intelligence and Its Measurement: A Symposium." *Journal of Educational Psychology,* 1921, *12,* 210–212.

Ferrara, R. A., Brown, A. L., and Campione, J. C. "Children's Learning and Transfer of Inductive Reasoning Rules: A Study of Proximal Development." Paper presented at the meeting of the Society for Research in Child Development, Boston, April 1981.

Ferrara, R. A., Brown, A. L., and Campione, J. C. "Children's Learning and Transfer Transfer of Inductive Reasoning Rules: A Study of Proximal Development." Unpublished manuscript, University of Illinois, 1983.

Feuerstein, R. *The Dynamic Assessment of Retarded Performers: The Learning Potential Assessment Device, Theory, Instruments, and Techniques.* Baltimore: University Park Press, 1979.

Palincsar, A. S., and Brown, A. L. "Reciprocal Teaching of Comprehension-Fostering and Monitoring Activities." *Cognition and Instruction,* in press.

Spearman, C. *The Nature of "Intelligence" and Principles of Cognition.* London: Macmillan, 1923.

Thorndike, E. L. *Measurement of Intelligence.* New York: Teachers College Press, 1926.

Vygotsky, L. S. *Mind in Society: The Development of Higher Psychological Processes.* Cambridge, Mass.: Harvard University Press, 1978.

Joseph Campione and Ann L. Brown are professors of psychology and education at the University of Illinois at Urbana-Champaign. Roberta A. Ferrara and Nancy R. Bryant are graduate students in the Department of Psychology at the University of Illinois at Urbana-Champaign.

What are the roles of consciousness and of collectivism in Vygotsky's theory?

Vygotsky's Zone of Proximal Development: The Hidden Agenda

Jerome Bruner

We must not lose sight of Vygotsky's philosophical commitment to Marxism or, more specifically, of Vygotsky's commitment to a psychology based on Marxist premises. Moreover, he was writing during the 1920s and 1930s, when Russian Marxist theory was orthodox, starchy, and heavy-handed. The lively revisionism of modern Marxist theory as represented by "Western" intellectuals, such as Lukacs, and by those who sought to refresh Marxism with an infusion of European phenomenology was nowhere in sight. The Russian party line was tied around Marxist thinking so tightly that it squeezed out the kinds of inquiry that interested Vygotsky in that early period and that were to preoccupy Marxist intellectuals (particularly outside Russia) in the decades following. So, when we think of Vygotsky's psychological theories, we must remember not only that he was a Marxist but that he was devoted to the intellectual freshening of Marxist doctrine. And, it is well known that his efforts on behalf of such refreshment eventually got him into deep trouble with the Russian ideologues in charge of official doctrine.

I see two strands in his writing that were "revolutionary" from the Marxist perspective of his time and place. His critics would surely have called these strands revisionist. The first has to do with the role of consciousness and of "mental events" in human affairs—a treacherous topic in a climate of historical materialism. For Vygotsky, consciousness loomed large, nowhere more

B. Rogoff, J. V. Wertsch (Eds.). *Children's Learning in the "Zone of Proximal Development."*
New Directions for Child Development, no. 23. San Francisco: Jossey-Bass, March 1984.

so than in his discussion of the zone of proximal development. The second strand relates to collectivism in its most generic sense: the manner in which goals are achieved in a socialist society. Recall that Vygotsky had been involved, along with Luria and others of his "friends" (they regarded themselves as students or at least as his juniors), in a study of the impact of collectivism on peasant thought. The principal finding of their study—suppressed for years, and finally appearing not in the form in which Vygotsky wrote it but only in Luria's book (1976) of many years later—was that participation in an agricultural collective had the effect of promoting growth in the thinking of the peasants involved, which took them from childlike, primitive forms of thinking to adult forms of thought. Collective activity, in a word, led peasants along the way to adult thinking or—better—to socialist adult thinking, which in Vygotsky's account was a more rational, more "scientific" form of thinking. Such was the dogmatic romanticism among the leading figures in the official Russian establishment of the time that they took Vygotsky's conclusion as a criticism of peasants for their prescientific thinking—and banned the book.

Reading Luria's (1976) account of the expedition that Vygotsky led to Uzbekistan and Kirghizia, which was composed many years later from his notes and which was written (so Luria assured me in conversation) in the spirit of Vygotsky's ideas of the earlier period, I was struck by the degree to which the "modernization" of peasant thought by collectivism was framed in the same language and the same theoretical mode as Vygotsky's discussion of the growth of the child from prescientific to scientific thinking. Luria most certainly discusses the precollective peasant as if he were a child in need of induction into the grown-up world of the collective farm. Indeed, when I had occasion to review Luria's book (Bruner, 1977), I commented on that parallel and made some critical remarks about the simplistic assumption that cultural change was like the growth of the child. I think I saw Luria only once again after I wrote that review, which I sent to him in Moscow. He said he had liked it, but he was not prepared to give up the Vygotskian idea of the parallel between modernization of the peasant and the growth of the child.

Let me now return to the main theme—the hidden agenda in Vygotsky's idea of the zone of proximal development (ZPD). I believe that the idea is a fusion of the idea of collectivism and of the role of consciousness. Indeed, as I see it, the ZPD is a direct expression of the way in which the division of labor expresses itself in a collectivist society. It involves a sharing not only of knowledge but of consciousness, albeit an historically shaped consciousness. Those who "know" more, those who have "higher" consciousness share it with those who know less, who are less developed in consciousness and intellectual control. Each in his or her time comes to have a mind shaped by the historical and economic circumstances of the period (and of history in general by extension), but the transmission of mind across history is effected not by blind material forces but by the form of mental sharing that we now know as the zone of proximal development. In the case of the growing child, it is made possible by parents and "more expert peers." In his famous discussion in *Thought and Language* (Vygotsky, 1962), of the replacement of initial "spontaneous" concepts by later "scientific" ones, this transmission is accomplished by instruction in school. In the case of the Uzbek peasant collective worker, it is brought about by direct participation in the more advanced technical life of the kolkhoz, in whose day-to-day processes of production and planning he participates. In each case, it is a matter of somebody with knowledge and awareness scaffolding a task for somebody without knowledge and awareness until the latter becomes capable of "reaching higher ground"—as in the celebrated discussion in *Thought and Language* of how the child is led from arithmetic to algebraic thinking or as in Luria's account of how the peasant is led from concrete thinking to a capacity to grasp broader, higher inferential principles.

Now, language serves exceptionally well in a Marxist theory of this kind as the medium both for collective sharing and for transmission of new forms of consciousness across generations and circumstances. In the first place, in Marxist and in other forms of theory, language is a historically conditioned instrument. Here, Vygotsky had in mind not only natural language but also the languages of science and mathematics—and the language or notational system in which economic activity is carried out under socialist and presocialist regimes. It is plain from the first discussion of the ZPD in *Thought and Language* that introduction into a new form of language and a new use of language (which themselves were produced by changed historical circumstances) alters the way in which the mind of the user will work. It is as if new forms of notation and the new distinctions contained within them are temptations to think in a manner concordant with the language—much as in the spirit of Sapir, Whorf, and earlier thinkers like Humboldt. The idea was very widespread among Russian linguists and literary intellectuals of the day, such as Bakhtin, Troubetskoy, and the young Roman Jakobson. Indeed, Jakobson has written vividly of the famous young professor of linguistics at Leningrad, the cosmopolitan Pole Baudouin de Courtenay, who by the turn of the twentieth century had already discussed the psychological reality of the phoneme, which had yet to be called that, and the obligatory psychological impact of linguistic distinctions. Vygotsky and Bakhtin knew of each other (Bakhtin most certainly admired Vygotsky), and it is just as unthinkable for an aspiring psycholinguist like Vygotsky not to have heard of the work of Baudouin de Courtenay as it would have been for Roger Brown in his early thirties not to have heard of the ideas of Benjamin Lee Whorf.

Recall, too, that in the decades after the Revolution the emphasis on literacy was so great that the recently literate were enjoined to go out and share their new skills—and new consciousness—with their less tutored brothers as barefoot literacy teachers. This expression of the new collectivism was a far less bureaucratic, far more Kropotkin-like idea than what prevails today in the "mature" socialist state.

Let me add one more point before I conclude. I owe this point to discussions with many thoughtful contemporary Marxists. Many comment on the fact that first Marx and later his followers were always concerned with a "principle of spontaneity" in Marxist theory. It is a means of conceiving the action of human beings as something not completely dominated by material and historical forces. In the first official revisions of psychological orthodoxy in Russia in the late 1930s, the principle of *gnost* was introduced by Bernstein— a concept like "effortful attention" that allows some responsibility for action to reside in the individual human being. Ushering in what Bauer (1952) considered a new conception of action, it spelled the beginning of "the new Soviet man." Responsibility no longer resided fully with history: Socialist society was making its own history, and if things went badly for the individual, one could not so simply name the society as the culprit. There is a curious anomaly, however, in placing the responsibility both on history and at the same time on the individual—whether on his *gnost,* his orienting reflexes, or something else.

This is where I think Vygotsky's brilliance as a Marxist thinker came to the fore. The principle of spontaneity that he was urging was not to be a throwback into individual psychology and noncollectivist ethics. Realization of one's individual powers through the utilization of knowledge and shared consciousness depended not on the individual child but on society's capacity to provide the child with the symbolic tools that the child needed in order to grow: on providing opportunity for the child to enter into relationship with somebody wiser or abler than himself who would provide the necessary concepts and consciousness that would enable him to make the epistemic leap forward that Vygotsky saw as the promise of the Revolution. The ZPD was its instrument.

So, while the major developmental thinker of capitalist Western Europe, Jean Piaget, set forth an image of human development as a lone venture for the child, in which others could not help unless the child had already figured things out on his own and in which not even language could provide useful hints about the conceptual matters to be mastered, the major developmentalist of socialist Eastern Europe set forth a view in which growth was a collective responsibility and language one of the major tools of that collectivity. Now, all these years later, Vygotsky's star is rising in the Western sky as Piaget's declines, while it is declining in the East (at least officially) where no new one is yet in sight.

I have one remaining conjecture. Vygotsky was a pioneer of "Marxist" psychology. There really are none to speak of before him. Pavlov was adopted by Marxists, although many thoughtful Marxists found his materialist psychology brassy and lacking in the subtlety of dialectical materialism. Curiously, it was a step away from his materialist base—to consideration of an historically based Second Signal System—that endeared Pavlov to the later budding Marxist psychological community that was already rejecting the crude materialism of the early years. An even more materialist predecessor of Pavlov, Bechterev, was even less admired by committed Marxists. His *Reflexology*

(1933) made even the most flagrant materialism of J. B. Watson seem rather mentalistic by comparison. So Vygotsky was very much on his own. He started a tradition that would be true both to the rather idealistic Marxism that he had embraced and to the literary-intellectual-linguistic tradition of Russia— a truly remarkable tradition that produced not only such linguistic greats as Jakobson, Troubetskoy, Propp, and Bakhtin but their poet friends, whose gifts and linguistic awareness we are just now coming to appreciate. The rejection of consciousness and inner language by crude Marxist polemicists was not for Vygotsky. Yet, he was faithful to the Marxist historical ideal in his own way. It is not surprising that discussion of the ZPD and how it manages to shape growing consciousness with the aid of language is at times opaque. In fact, Vygotsky was muddling through as best he could. Reading him today, one cannot escape the feeling that, for a man at the head of a procession that he must at times have doubted would ever form, he did astonishingly well.

References

Bauer, R. A. *The New Man in Soviet Psychology.* Cambridge, Mass.: Harvard University Press, 1952.

Bechterev, V. M. *General Principles of Human Reflexology.* New York: International Publishers, 1933.

Bruner, J. S. "Peasants to Tractor Drivers: Review of A. R. Luria's *Cognitive Psychology.*" *Nature,* 1977, *268* (5621), 672.

Luria, A. R. *Cognitive Development: Its Cultural and Social Foundations.* Cambridge, Mass.: Harvard University Press, 1976.

Vygotsky, L. S. *Thought and Language.* Cambridge, Mass.: M.I.T. Press, 1962.

Jerome Bruner is George Herbert Mead Professor at the New School for Social Research, New York.

Index